# 10
# DISCOVERIES
# ON YOUR
# ROAD TO
# GREATNESS

# RICH WILKERSON

Published by

LIFEBRIDGE
B O O K S
P.O. BOX 49428
CHARLOTTE, NC 28277

Printed in the United States of America.

*To my parents,*
*John and Bonnie Wilkerson,*
*who introduced me to the*
*"Ten Discoveries" early in life.*
*I love you both.*

# CONTENTS

# HELP!
# I'M INSIGNIFICANT!

The definition of the word insignificant is: too small to be important – without weight or influence. Wow! Have you ever felt like that? Do you feel that way right now?

Moses writes the following – which comes from the mouth of God Himself: *"Then God said let us make man in our image, in our likeness and let them rule over the fish of the sea, the birds of the air, over the livestock and over all the earth and over all the creatures that move along the ground. God created man in his own image. In the image of God he created him"* (Genesis 1:26-27).

Whether you feel insignificant or not, the truth is: YOU WERE BORN FOR GREATNESS!

Other than "The Fonz," I don't know anyone more

arrogant and prideful on American television than George Jefferson. Do you remember the little guy married to "Weezie," whose theme song was, *Well, we're moving on up to the East Side; to a deluxe apartment in the sky*?

George Jefferson was the owner of a dry cleaners in Manhattan. He was well-to-do, had defied the odds and was incredibly funny. Yet we must admit, he was also extremely arrogant!

While God doesn't want us to feel insignificant, He doesn't want us to be arrogant either. Instead, the Lord desires that we have the big picture of who He is and to know we are made in His image – we have God's greatness stamped all over our DNA. He longs for us to be liberated from "small thinking" and for the debilitating feeling of insignificance to be completely obliterated from our lives.

The Creator desires that you declare these words again and again:

> *"I was made in the image of God.*
> *I may look like my earthly father and mother, but I have my Heavenly Father's greatness in me.*
> *I was born to make a difference.*
> *I was born to lift people higher than they believe they can go.*
> *I was born to win.*
> *I was born to plunder hell in order to populate heaven.*
> *I was born to be at the top and not at the bottom.*
> *I was born to be the head and not the tail.*

*Since I was made in the image of God, the
potential for greatness is rooted in me."*

We are all born for *great* vision, *great* family, *great* accomplishment and a *great* life. Sadly, however, many have settled for mediocrity. Why? I believe too many people are haunted by a feeling of inadequacy. They complain, "Oh, I am not important. I'm nothing."

Let me list "10 Maybes" that help produce the spirit of insignificance in a person's life:

1. Maybe you come from a broken family.
2. Maybe you had nine brothers and sisters, and you thought you were just another kid.
3. Maybe you were raised under "So and So's" shadow.
4. Maybe you've been told repeatedly by people you love that you are useless.
5. Maybe you were sexually abused as a child
6. Maybe you have a physical handicap.
7. Maybe you're an immigrant and have had a difficult time adjusting to your new country.
8. Maybe you are an orphan and have felt unloved.
9. Maybe extreme poverty has made you feel worthless!
10. Maybe – just maybe – you haven't given God a chance to help you.

The question remains: "How can I get rid of this feeling of *smallness* in my life?"

You may say, "Of course, I want to be the person God wants me to be, but Rich Wilkerson, I just don't view life the way you do. You can't possibly know what I've been through. Yes, I want to share in God's big picture – and desire what you're talking about. But please help me – I feel so inferior, so insignificant!"

In the next ten chapters I'm going to give you "10 DISCOVERIES" that will help propel you ON YOUR ROAD TO GREATNESS. They are based on what God delivered to Moses centuries ago on Mount Sinai.

At the end of this book there are four decisions I want you to prayerfully consider. If you faithfully make these a daily priority, you will move FROM INSIGNIFICANT TO GREAT! I promise.

*– Rich Wilkerson*

# THERE CAN ONLY BE ONE "NUMBER ONE!"

*He is a self-made man who worships his creator.*

– JOHN BRIGHT

What a reality-check to be in the presence of ego-driven people! You know who I'm talking about – those who mistakenly believe the world orbits around their decisions and jumps at their commands.

These individuals worship at the feet of what I call the "unholy trinity" of Me, Myself and I.

The Bible clearly tells us we were made in the likeness and image of the Creator, however, if we are not careful, conceit creeps in. We glance in the mirror and think, "Lord, You're looking good today!"

Wait just a minute! You're not God. You were made

to be *like* Him, yet it must always be the Almighty we worship – not ourselves!

The self-centered express their focus of life when they exclaim: "I need more stuff," "I want to feel good," or "Just as long as I'm happy!" They are ruled and motivated by feelings, desires and lust – ingredients that can lead to destruction.

> *The self-centered express their focus of life when they exclaim: "I need more stuff," or I want to feel good."*

Do you recall the Old Testament story of Nebuchadnezzar, a king who was full of his own importance? One day as he stood on the balcony of his palace – somewhere in what is now Iraq – he bragged, *"Is not this the great Babylon I have built as the royal residence, by my mighty power and for the glory of my majesty?"* (Daniel 4:30).

At that moment God struck him and the king lost his sanity. The Bible records that for seven years he was driven into the field like a homeless person, eating grass like cattle. *His body was drenched with the dew of heaven until his hair grew like the feathers of an eagle and his nails like the claws of a bird* (v.33).

Finally, Nebuchadnezzar came to his senses and acknowledged that the Most High God is sovereign over the kingdoms of men and He gives them to anyone He wishes. After his confession, the king raised his eyes toward heaven and his *"sanity was restored"* (v.34).

Nebuchadnezzar learned the hard way there can only be *one* "Number One!"

## A DIVINE MANDATE

Life hits all of us at break-neck speed. Isn't it time to step back a few paces and take a wider look? Who is really in charge? Is it you, or someone far greater?

On mount Sinai, in a voice like thunder, the Almighty delivered to Moses His divine mandate – the Ten Commandments:

*And God spoke all these words: "I am the Lord your God, who brought you out of Egypt, out of the land of slavery. You shall have no other gods before me."*
EXODUS 20:1-3

What a powerful statement! God began with three profound announcements:

1. He tells us who He is – "I am the Lord."
2. He speaks of His relationship to us – "the Lord *your* God."
3. He declares what He has done for us – He "brought you out of Egypt." The slavery of Pharaoh represents Satan's kingdom.

Look what our Father has done! He has rescued us from the kingdom of darkness and brought us into His marvelous light. That is why He asks us to embrace the First Commandment: *"You shall have no other God's before me."*

## SMOKE ON THE MOUNTAIN!

Can you imagine what it must have been like for the children of Israel to be gazing up on the mountain when the commandments were delivered? Actually, we don't have to wonder. The Bible tells precisely what occurred as Moses was hearing from God: *When the people saw the thunder and lightning and heard the trumpet and saw the mountain in smoke, they trembled with fear. They stayed at a distance and said to Moses, "Speak to us yourself and we will listen. But do not have God speak to us or we will die"* (Exodus 20:18-19).

Immediately, Moses tried to calm the multitude, saying, *"Do not be afraid. God has come to test you, so that the fear of God will be with you to keep you from sinning"* (v.20).

**Godly fear is the beginning of wisdom.**

The moment the people heard the command, a wave of anxiety swept over them. As first-hand witnesses they were acutely aware that God's presence is awesome and holy – and it caused them to tremble.

The fear Moses spoke of can only be described as "unending respect." Total reverence and honor for Almighty God would keep them from iniquity.

**When you fear God first, there's no reason to dread anything else!**

The greatest exchange you'll ever make is when you

trade your anxiety for a healthy fear of the Lord. Suddenly, there's no need to be afraid in the midst of a financial crunch or a health crisis. You'll stop worrying whether your car is going to run off the road or if your children will dabble in drugs. Instead, you reverently fear the Great Jehovah – not just the temporal things of this world!

## GOD – AND GOD ALONE!

When the Creator commands, "You shall have no other God's before Me!" He is saying:

- Your son or daughter is not your god!
- Your career is not your god!
- Your hobby is not your god!
- Your sport is not your god!

There is only one true God – the Maker of all things. If you fail to accept this as divine truth you will – over time – create your own gods to gratify your selfish purposes.

That's exactly what the Greeks did. Before marching into battle, they would worship Zeus, their god of power. If they were about to indulge in a night of eating and drinking, they would pray to Bacchus, their god of gluttony and excess. Before nights of orgies, they bowed

*There is only one true God – the Maker of all things.*

before Aphrodite, their godess of love.

The people of Athens were astonished when the apostle Paul stood before them and proclaimed: *"I see that in every way you are very religious. For as I walked around and looked carefully at your objects of worship, I even found an altar with this inscription: TO AN UNKNOWN GOD. Now what you worship as something unknown I am going to proclaim to you"* (Acts 17:22-23).

Paul then told them of the only God – the One who made the world and everything in it: the *"Lord of heaven and earth [who] does not live in temples built by hands"* (v.24).

## A WORLD OF FALSE GODS

The list of counterfeit deities is endless – spanning everything from drugs and dogma to pleasure and philosophy. Here are three substitutes that should arouse your suspicion and raise red flags:

## 1. Beware of the gods of false religions and cults.

You are at the airport, waiting for your plane to leave, when a pleasant young man walks up and asks, "Can I talk with you for a moment?"

The doorbell rings and two well-dressed women are standing on your doorstep – eager to hand you some literature.

Rather than be lured into their trap of deception, walk

away or politely ask them to leave. More than likely they are wolves in sheep's clothing with only one objective: to entice you into their man-made religion.

Here's the one question such people dread to hear: "Is faith in Jesus Christ the only way by which a person can receive salvation and make it to heaven?"

You see, cults and false religions do not believe in the divinity of Christ. Instead, they present a works-based plan that ties people to the cause. And, almost always, the pronouncement of their leader carries more weight than scripture.

Rather than serving God, they want the Lord to serve them, magnifying their misguided beliefs.

Don't just walk away – run!

*When you consult astrological charts you open your mind to demonic influence.*

## 2. Beware of the false god called astrology.

I was shocked when a Christian woman was praising God because she was going to have a great day – "I read it in my horoscope this morning in the newspaper" she exclaimed!

Let me put it bluntly: when you consult astrological charts you open your mind to demonic influence.

God warns those who *"worshiped other gods, bowing down to them or to the sun or the moon or the stars of the sky"* (Deuteronomy 17:3).

17

Here is what the Lord says to the residents of Babylon: *"Let your astrologers come forward, those stargazers who make predictions month by month, let them save you from what is coming upon you. Surely they are like stubble; the fire will burn them up. They cannot even save themselves from the power of the flame"* (Isaiah 47:13-14).

You don't need the Zodiac to forecast your future when it is revealed to us by God's Spirit (1 Corinthians 2:10).

## 3. Beware of the false gods of music, sports and entertainment.

Culture has redefined the meaning of worship. Today, millions of young people are obsessed by rock stars, emulating their fashions, language and behavior – with little regard for where the road may lead.

> *God's Word says, "their rock is not like our Rock."*
> DEUTERONOMY 32:31.

"Oh, I love the music," is no excuse to bow at the feet of those whose deity is drugs and whose lord is lust. Why would anyone want to pattern their life after Janis Joplin, Jimmy Hendrix or Kurt Cobain? Don't they see the tragedy that lies ahead?

Remember, God's Word says, *"their rock is not like our Rock"* (Deuteronomy 32:31).

The problem is not only with teens. I've met born-again housewives who know ten times more about Tom

Cruise than the works of the apostles – Peter, James or John.

Dad's aren't exempt – most seem far more excited over the Super Bowl than scripture.

Take an inventory of your priorities. The Bible gives this warning: *"There is a way that seems right to a man, but in the end it leads to death"* (Proverbs 14:12).

## Rise Above Yourself

I encounter people who constantly create false gods to serve their selfish desires. However, they will never rise above themselves if what they worship is simply a visible expression of the human qualities they already possess.

When you sow to the gods of this world, you will only reap what the Bible calls "the works of the flesh" – *sexual immorality, impurity and debauchery; idolatry and witchcraft; hatred, discord, jealousy, fits of rage, selfish ambition, dissensions, factions and envy; drunkenness, orgies, and the like* (Galatians 5:19-21).

It's time to set your sight on things above – to worship the only God who can give you the fruit of the Spirit – *love, joy, peace, patience, kindness, goodness, faithfulness, gentleness and self-control* (Galatians 5:22-23).

When you prayerfully ask the Lord for these characteristics, by His mercy and grace He will give you even more. You will receive knowledge, wisdom, abundance and power from on high! Don't settle for less

19

than Jesus came to provide.

Those who invite the one true God into their lives will experience far more than 15 minutes of fleeting fame. Your day is coming! As you enter heaven, the angels will roll out the red carpet and herald your arrival. Your Father knows all about you – and you are going to spend eternity with Him.

## "Most Important"

The First Commandment is more than a directive of the Old Testament. One day, when Jesus was debating with religious leaders, a teacher of the law asked Him, *"Of all the commandments, which is the most important?"* (Mark 12:28).

Jesus replied: *"The most important one...is this: 'Hear, O Israel, the Lord our God, the Lord is one. Love the Lord your God with all your heart and with all your soul and with all your mind and with all your strength'"* (vv. 29-30).

This was a positive restatement of the Almighty telling us: "You shall have no other God's before Me."

The name of Jehovah in Hebrew is Yahweh – meaning the one who "was" and "is" and "always will be." He has no beginning and will have no ending. Our God is:

- Omnipotent – all powerful.
- Omnipresent – everywhere at the same time.
- Omniscient – He knows all things knowable.

That is why today and *everyday* in heaven, the angels never stop praising: *"Holy, holy, holy is the Lord God Almighty, who was, and is, and is to come"* (Revelation 4:8).

Hallelujah! Your God is incomparable, unequaled, and rightfully deserves first place in your life.

---

## DECISIONS

*Have certain activities become "number one" in my life?*

*How can I be certain that God has top priority?*

*How is "the fear of the Lord" demonstrated in my daily walk?*

---

# DISCOVERY 2

# LOVE WHAT'S REAL – NOT A SUBSTITUTE

*Men are idol factories.*
– JOHN CALVIN

One day shopping at the mall, I heard a mom loudly scolding her rambunctious five-year-old son: "If you do that one more time, you're going to be in big trouble!"

Not 30 seconds later, the woman threatened again: "Did you hear me? If you keep that up I'm going to punish you big time!"

Evidently, the boy had heard those words before and they were more bark than bite. That's why he continued to act up.

Thankfully, God doesn't operate like some parents. When He gives a directive, He means it – and does not have to tell you twice.

Read what happened when Moses first told the people

23

of the Lord's words and laws. The Bible records *"they responded with one voice, 'Everything the Lord has said we will do'"* (Exodus 24:3).

But would they? Let's take a look at the Second Commandment:

> *You shall not make for yourself an idol in the form*
> *of anything in heaven above or on the earth beneath*
> *or in the waters below. You shall not bow down to them*
> *or worship them; for I, the Lord your God, am a jealous*
> *God, punishing the children for the sin of the fathers*
> *to the third and fourth generation of those who hate*
> *me, but showing love to a thousand generations of*
> *those who love me and keep my commandments.*
>
> EXODUS 20:4-6

What a short memory the Israelites had. It almost defies imagination. While Moses was on top of Mount Sinai receiving the commandments, the people were down below blatantly disobeying them!

God had declared: "No graven images!" yet that's exactly what the children of Israel were making.

Since Moses had been gone 40 days, the restless people gathered around his brother, Aaron, and said, *"Come, make us gods who will go before us. As for this fellow Moses who brought us up out of Egypt, we don't know what has happened to him"* (Exodus 21:1).

Aaron was more than willing to oblige. He told the throng, *"Take off the gold earrings that your wives, your sons and your daughters are wearing, and bring them to me"* (v.2).

He gathered what they gave him and fashioned an idol shaped like a calf. Then he said, *"These are your gods, O Israel, who brought you up out of Egypt"* (v.4).

The Israelis were used to God speaking – and miracles happening. So, while Moses was waiting on the Lord, they were impatiently saying, "We need gods right now!"

> They threw their gold into a hot pot and let Aaron shape it into an object of worship.

That's why they threw their gold into a hot pot and let Aaron shape it into an object of worship – believing this is what delivered them from bondage!

The golden calf was man made, yet they eagerly bowed before it. The next day they even had a festival and sacrificed burnt offerings to their new idol.

God saw what was happening and told Moses, *"Go down, because your people, whom you brought up out of Egypt, have become corrupt. They have been quick to turn away from what I commanded them and have made themselves an idol cast in the shape of a calf"* (v.7).

Up on Mount Sinai, the Lord gave Moses the commandments in writing: *"...two tablets of the Testimony, the tablets of stone inscribed by the finger of God"* (Exodus 31:18).

With the etched tablets in hand, Moses walked into the camp and saw the people dancing before the golden image. The Bible tells us that *"his anger burned and he threw the tablets out of his hands, breaking them to pieces at the foot of the mountain"* (v.19). He took the calf they had made and burned it in the fire; then he ground it to powder, scattered it on the water and made the Israelites drink it (v.20).

Following their disobedience, you can read how *"the Lord struck the people with a plague"* (v.35).

> *If we begin using an image to help us worship, we eventually rely upon and worship the object itself.*

## HELPLESS IDOLS

Why does the Lord forbid the carving or sculpting of idols? Because He knows that if we begin using an image to help us worship, we eventually rely upon and worship the object itself.

Here are four reasons we must avoid using graven images:

### 1. All idols are man made.

When you have a life-changing experience with the true and living God, there's no need for a substitute. That's why, many years later, King David could write: *"But their idols are silver and gold, made by the hands of men.*

26

*They have mouths, but cannot speak, eyes, but they cannot see; they have ears, but cannot hear, noses, but they cannot smell; they have hands, but cannot feel, feet, but they cannot walk; nor can they utter a sound with their throats"* (Psalm 115:4-7).

Here is what the Almighty says about those who have *"provoked me to anger by all the idols their hands have made"* (2 Kings 22:17). He declares that His *"anger will burn...and will not be quenched"* (v.17).

## 2. Idols have no ability to communicate.

I love the story of the face-off between Elijah and the 450 idol-worshiping prophets of Baal. It was a contest on Mount Carmel to answer the question: "Who is the real God?" In the confrontation, He would be the one to answer by fire.

The Bible says the prophets of Baal placed a bull on the altar of sacrifice and called on the name of their god from morning until noon. *"'O Baal, answer us!' they shouted. But there was no response; no one answered. And they danced around the altar they had made"* (1 Kings 18:26).

Then Elijah began to taunt them. *"Shout louder!"* he said. *"Surely he is a god! Perhaps he is deep in thought, or busy, or traveling. Maybe he is sleeping and must be awakened"* (v.27).

In a frenzy, they cried out and slashed themselves with swords and spears until their blood flowed (v.28). The men continued their frantic prophesying until the time for the evening sacrifice. Still there was no response from their supposed god.

Now came Elijah's turn. He repaired the altar, then called on the God of Abraham, Isaac and Israel and miraculously, the fire fell. When the people witnessed what happened, *they fell prostrate and cried, "The Lord – he is God! The Lord – he is God!"* (v.39).

Friend, you can yell and scream at your man-made objects of worship from now until eternity, but remember a piece of wood or a chunk of stone is never going to respond. Only God Almighty can hear and answer your plea.

## 3. Idols are lifeless.

Even today, there are Christians worldwide attending churches and cathedrals who still rub their hands on statues of saints. Their motives may be pure, but what they are touching is cold and impersonal. That's why the apostle Paul states: *"Therefore since we are God's offspring, we should not think that the divine being is like gold or silver or stone – an image made by man's design and skill"* (Acts 17:29).

I'm happy to report that our God is very much alive!

## 4. Man-made idols must have human support in order to be sustained.

Let me share a little secret. When an idol gets dirty, it

can't wash itself. If the paint fades or becomes chipped, a human has to repaint and restore it. And what happens if an arm falls off? Somebody else has to glue it back on!

The statue is totally helpless!

Yet, even to this day, if such an idol falls on its face, some dear soul will prop it back up and then have the belief to say: "Now, can you help me?"

Of course, it can't because it has no power.

My friend, that's not the kind of deity I wish to serve.

## An Easy Choice

Who will you worship? The all-knowing, all-powerful, ever-present God, or a lifeless piece of sculptured rock or an inanimate carved piece of wood.

In the Old Testament you read about armies who invaded hostile territories and smashed the idols of the enemy. Thank God, we serve Jehovah – who has never lost a battle or been overthrown.

*We serve Jehovah – who has never lost a battle or been overthrown.*

Instead, He knows *in advance* how victory will come.

When God sent the ten plagues on Pharaoh, each was at one time an idol to the Egyptians. They worshiped frogs, locusts – even blood. Yet the Almighty took care of those ancient gods one by one. Then He released His people so there would be no doubt that Jehovah reigns.

## The Money God

You may be quick to say, "I don't worship a graven image!"

Are you absolutely sure? Just how important is that engraved coin in your pocket or purse? What's the value you place on a stock certificate or a $1,000 bill?

I am convinced that America's number one graven image is money.

We hear about "buying power" but let me tell you what money can and *cannot* buy:

- It can buy books but not brains.
- It can buy libraries but not knowledge.
- It can buy a wedding but not a marriage.
- It can buy you a house but not a home.
- It can buy a new heart transplant but it can't buy forgiveness.
- It can buy a sanctuary but not a Savior.
- It can buy hell, but can never gain you entry into heaven.

Friend, money is paper, or simply a number on a bank computer screen. It is lifeless – and the only power it has is what we give it.

As many learn the hard way, it is easily destroyed. In the recent "dot com crash" many Americans lost over half of their net worth in a short span of time. In reality, it doesn't take much to deplete a bank account when all that backs it up is a love for wealth.

In the right hands, money can accomplish great works. It can feed the poor, help those who are sick – even spread the Gospel of Christ.

Instead of loving the almighty dollar, love the One who owns the cattle on a thousand hills – all the oil, gold, silver and precious stones on the planet. He is the Creator who made everything with His own hands.

Money, however, is man's invention.

Jesus tells us: *"No one can serve two masters. Either he will hate the one and love the other, or he will be devoted to the one and despise the other. You cannot serve both God and Money"* (Matthew 6:24).

*What you truly love determines your future – not only yours, but that of your entire family.*

### TRUE WORSHIP

Let me remind you that when the Lord gave the Second Commandment He said, *"I am a jealous God."* Even more, He spoke of *"punishing the children for the sin of the fathers to the third and fourth generation of those who hate me."*

That's why I believe what you truly love determines your future – not only *yours*, but that of your entire family. God demands all praise, all glory and all allegiance.

Through the centuries, in a futile attempt to visualize a higher power, man has created gods of brass, steel, wood, stone – and even paper. But here's what the Lord wants you to know: *"Yet a time is coming and has now come when the true worshipers will worship the Father in spirit and truth, for they are the kind of worshipers the Father seeks. God is spirit, and his worshipers must worship in spirit and in truth"* (John 4:23-24).

When the Lord takes residence in your heart, you'll no longer need a substitute. Rejoice in the assurance you are now a child of the *one and only* living God.

DECISIONS

*What are the "graven images" of our culture?*

*What steps am I taking to avoid worshiping such objects?*

*How can I demonstrate that my view and God's view of money is the same?*

# DISCOVERY 3

# YOUR WORDS ARE A REFLECTION OF YOUR HEART

*Profanity is the use of strong words by weak people.*
– E.C. MCKENZIE

Most parents chastize their children for cursing, but in the home where I was raised, the list of banned words was long indeed. For example, we weren't allowed to say "gosh, darn, heck or gee" – those were just substitutes for "God, damn, hell or Jesus!"

I can still remember what happened when I uttered one of those forbidden words. My mom would take a washcloth, dip it in hot water and soap and say: "Open you mouth, son. There's some filth in there and we are going to get it out!"

Other times she would scrub my tongue with a brush!

We couldn't even say, "Shut up!" – that was almost as bad as cursing God's Name.

Today, I thank the Lord for the standards set by my parents, and Robyn and I have done our best to pass those same values down to our own children – to keep both their hearts and their mouths pure.

I laugh when I think of the time our son, Richie, was about five years old. He couldn't say his "s's" – and pronounced them as "f's""

One afternoon he came running in the house from playing ball outside with a little girl next door who was named Christina. "Dad, you know what Chriftina 'faid?"

*I thank the Lord for the standards set by my parents, and Robyn and I have done our best to pass those same values down to our own children.*

"What was that," I answered.

"Fee faid, 'Fut up!' And I faid to her "Chriftina you foudn't fay 'Fut up!' Jefuf doefn't like it when you fay 'Fut up!' But fee faid 'Fut up' anyway!"

Stifling a smile, I replied, "Son, you did the right thing. Everybody should be very careful what they say."

## OH! WHAT A NAME!

From every side we're bombarded with a constant barrage of foul language – in pop music, magazines, movies and television. And, far too often, it creeps into our own homes. Yet, we live under a mandate from God Himself not to take His name in vain. He issued the edict in the Third Commandment:

> *You shall not misuse the name of the Lord your God, for the Lord will not hold anyone guiltless who misuses his name.*
>
> EXODUS 20:7

This is the first and *only* commandment that includes an immediate threat of punishment – we won't be held guiltless. In other words, if we say "God" or "Jesus Christ" in a profane manner, we'd better be ready for the consequences.

Why does the Lord place such emphasis on this issue? To understand the reason, we need to know what the Father's name truly means. When you say "God," you are not merely uttering a three-letter word. It encompasses so much more.

For example, in Hebrew His name is *Eloheim* – meaning the Only Supreme and True God. He is also called *El Shaddai* – God Almighty, One with absolutely no limitations.

### You're using the name of the Great "I AM!"

In the natural, God had given Moses what seemed an

impossible task. He was to lead millions of people out of the slavery of Egypt, yet on whose authority was he speaking? Why should the children of Israel follow him?

Even Moses had questions. He said to God, *"Suppose I go to the Israelites and say to them, 'The God of your fathers has sent me to you,' and they ask me, 'What is his name?' Then what shall I tell them?"* (Exodus 3:13).

The Almighty responded: *"I AM WHO I AM. This is what you are to say to the Israelites: 'I AM has sent me to you'"* (v.14). And He added, *"Say to the Israelites, 'The Lord, the God of your fathers – the God of Abraham, the God of Isaac and the God of Jacob – has sent me to you.' This is my name forever, the name by which I am to be remembered from generation to generation"* (v.15).

With authority, Moses was speaking on behalf of the God of the patriarchs – the One who preceded these great men. Jehovah *is*, meaning He has no beginning and no ending.

When you speak the name of God or Jesus Christ, you are uttering the Hebrew word *Yahweh,* which means "My Lord."

Centuries later, the apostle Paul wrote this about Jesus: *"Therefore God exalted him to the highest place and gave him the name that is above every name, that at the name of Jesus every knee should bow, in heaven and on earth and under the earth, and every tongue confess that Jesus Christ is Lord, to the glory of God the Father"* (Philippians 2:9-11).

What a powerful name!

Every time you speak the words "God" or "Jesus Christ," take a moment to reflect on who He is:

### He is Jehovah Elyon – your God Most High.

When I address the Lord, I pull my shoulders back and raise my head – even my hands are lifted. He is *El Elyon*, The Most High God who demands that I look up.

King David writes: *"I will be glad and rejoice in you; I will sing praise to your name, O Most High"* (Psalms 9:2).

*El Elyon!* How could you possibly blaspheme such a God?

### He is Jehovah Nissi – your Banner.

During a great battle fought by Joshua, as long as Moses held up his hands, the Israelites were winning. When he grew tired, others raised his hands for him to assure total victory (Exodus 17:10-13). After the conflict ended, *"Moses built an altar and called it The Lord is my Banner"* (v.15).

> *The Lord is our Helper – the One who covers and sustains us.*

Yesterday, today and forever, the Lord is our Helper, the One who covers and sustains us.

When God's Son was about to return to heaven, He promised to send another Helper – the Holy Spirit. He declared: *"And I will ask the Father, and he will give you another Counselor to be with you forever – the Spirit of truth. The world cannot accept him, because it neither sees him nor knows him. But you know him, for he lives with you and will be in you"* (John 14:16-17).

He is always there, interceding for us.

*Yahweh Nissi!* Your Banner. Why would you curse your God and Helper?

## He is Jehovah Sabaoth – your Protector.

The Lord is our Shield, our Guardian and Defender. He says: *"Fear not, for I have redeemed you; I have summoned you by name; you are mine. When you pass through the waters, I will be with you; and when you pass through the rivers, they will not sweep over you. When you walk through the fire, you will not be burned; the flames will not set you ablaze. For I am the Lord, your God, the Holy One of Israel, your Savior"* (Isaiah 43:1-3).

What a safety net! As God's child, your Father is constantly watching out for you.

*Yahweh Sabaoth!* How could you possibly swear at your Protector?

## He is Jehovah Shalom – your Peace.

Even in great turmoil, God's name must never be spoken in anger or wrath. Be like Gideon, who *"built an altar to the Lord...and called it The Lord is Peace"* (Judges 6:24).

Once, when the winds and waves were raging and the disciples were fearing for their very lives, it was Jesus who rose at the stern of the ship, reached His hand across the waters and said to the wind and waves, *"Peace, be still"* (Mark 4:39). And in that moment the howling winds subsided and the waves calmed. What a loving, peaceful God we serve!

As Paul the apostle declares: *"But now in Christ Jesus you who once were far away have been brought near through the blood of Christ. For he himself is our peace"* (Ephesians 2:13-14).

*Yahweh Shalom!* Why would you take the name of a Peacemaker in vain?

## He is Jehovah Tsidkenu – your Righteousness.

The Bible tells us: *"and this is his name whereby he shall be called, The Lord Our Righteousness"* (Jeremiah 23:6).

*By God's grace, I have been forgiven and am no longer exposed to the devil's assaults.*

Before I accepted Christ as my Savior, I was nothing but a sinner – naked before Satan and his attacks, with nothing to protect me. Then Jesus came and placed a covering of righteousness around my shoulders.

By God's grace I have been forgiven and am no longer exposed to the devil's assaults. I stand dressed in the

Lord's divine armor, complete in Him.

I can say with the prophets of old: *"I delight greatly in the Lord; my soul rejoices in my God. For he has clothed me with garments of salvation and arrayed me in a robe of righteousness"* (Isaiah 61:10).

*Yahweh Tsidkenu!* How can you ever desecrate His precious name by profanity?

**He is Jehovah Jireh – your Provider.**

*Are you sick? He comes with healing in His wings? Are you despondent? He will bring unspeakable joy.*

The Lord gave Abraham the ultimate test when He asked him to place his son, Isaac, on an altar of sacrifice. Instead of cursing God, the man who would become the "Father of all nations" followed the Lord's command.

At the final moment, just before Isaac was to be slain, God saw the heart of Abraham and supplied a substitute – a lamb to be sacrificed. *"So Abraham called that place The Lord Will Provide"* (Genesis 22:14).

Today, what do you need? Are you sick? He comes with healing in His wings? Are you despondent? He brings unspeakable joy. Are you destitute? Your provider owns the whole planet!

Paul said to young Timothy: *"Command those who are*

rich in this present world not to be arrogant nor to put their hope in wealth, which is so uncertain, but to put their hope in God, who richly provides us with everything for our enjoyment" (1 Timothy 6:17).

*Yahweh Jireh!* Instead of cursing, start *praising* your Provider.

## He is Jehovah Shammah – your Ever-Present Lord.

Our God is always there!

- In your most difficult trials.
- When you feel isolated and alone.
- When your family is far from home.
- When you feel rejected.

The Lord says: *"Never will I leave you; never will I forsake you"* (Hebrews 13:5).

God is with you – constantly by your side.

David asked, *"Where can I go from your Spirit? Where can I flee from your presence? If I go up to the heavens, you are there; if I make my bed in the depths, you are there. If I rise on the wings of the dawn, if I settle on the far side of the sea, even there your hand will guide me, your right hand will hold me fast"* (Psalms 139:7-10).

*Yahweh Shammah!* Would you be foolish enough to curse your Faithful Friend, your Ever-Present Lord?

## FROM CURSING TO BLESSING

When you listen to some people, you would think His name was "Damn it" – since those are the two words they constantly add to the name of God.

Dear friend, only He has the authority to damn anyone – not you, and not me. He is Holy and Altogether Lovely, and our words must reflect His greatness.

What power there is in speaking God's name! In just one word you are saying all of these things:

- My Helper.
- My Protector.
- My Peace.
- My Righteousness.
- My Provider.
- My Ever-Present Lord.

If you are ever tempted to misuse the Lord's name, consider these truths:

**If there is no respect for God there will be no respect for one's fellow man.**

I constantly hear young people using the word *disrespect* – "She disrespected me!"

It's time to deep-six that word from your vocabulary. Why? Because what you are saying is "I should be respected!"

The term only came into vogue when human beings decided they were something special. In truth, however, only God deserves our honor and great esteem.

The Bible reminds us that no matter what our status in life, *"for dust you are and to dust you will return"* (Genesis 3:19).

I am only a representative of Jesus Christ, My Lord and Savior. Outside of Him I am nothing – I have no worth. If it helps you to curse me – if somehow that would make you feel better – then go right ahead! Because it is not an issue whether you honor *me* or not, the question is: do you respect the King of Kings? However, if you esteem the Father, you will also desire to respect His sons and daughters.

*The person who shows a lack of respect toward his fellow man is usually the same individual who is quick to misuse the name of God or the Lord Jesus Christ.*

Far too often, we get the cart before the horse. The person who shows a lack of respect toward his fellow man is usually the same individual who is quick to misuse the name of God or the Lord Jesus Christ.

If you truly love the Lord, you will love your fellow man – which settles the issue of respect.

**When you curse God's name you are pointing the finger at the wrong person.**

I've heard young people who, when they get an "F" in high school or university, blame God – using His name as profanity. Wait a moment! It wasn't God who stayed up all night partying instead of studying. You cursed the wrong person!

Some people, after being given a ticket for speeding, as soon as the officer walks away, explode with a torrent of foul language: "God #@&%!" Hey, it wasn't God who had the lead foot!

Read the story of Job – a man whom the Lord allowed to be tested and tried by Satan. Job's wife was so frustrated that she looked at him and said, "Why don't you just curse God and die?" (Job 2:9).

Thankfully, Job didn't heed her advice. Instead, he declared: *"Though he slay me, yet will I hope in him"* (Job 13:15).

**When you choose to curse, you miss the God-given opportunity to bless.**

Research shows us that the only effective way to get rid of a bad habit is to exchange the negative with something positive. Since this is the case, we need to replace cursing with blessing.

If you want to see a dramatic change, start practicing the directive of Christ: *"Bless those who curse you, pray for* those who mistreat you" (Luke 6:28). *"Then your reward will be great, and you will be sons of the Most High"* (v.35).

Cursing is the easy way out. There's something far more worthwhile and beneficial. Blessing brings victory on earth and eternal reward in heaven.

Jesus says: *"No good tree bears bad fruit, nor does a bad tree bear good fruit. Each tree is recognized by its own fruit. People do not pick figs from thornbushes, or grapes from briers. The good man brings good things out of the good stored up in his heart, and the evil man brings evil things out of the evil stored up in his heart. For out of the overflow of his heart his mouth speaks"* (Luke 6:43-45).

Ask the Lord to cleanse and purify you. Repeat the prayer of David: *"Set a guard over my mouth, O Lord; keep watch over the door of my lips"* (Psalms 141:3).

Today, make a commitment to God that you are going to live by the Third Commandment – to control your words, rid your mouth of unbecoming language and never misuse His Holy name.

DECISIONS

*Are there words in your vocabulary you know the Lord is not pleased with?*

*What commitment will you make to the Lord regarding your speech?*

*What names of God have special meaning in your relationship with Him?*

# TAKING A BREAK ON SUNDAY IS AN ORDER!

*Do not let Sunday be taken from you.*
*If your soul has no Sunday, it becomes an orphan.*
— ALBERT SCHWEITZER

Hardly a day goes by when I don't say, "If I just had a little more time."

Technology promised modern conveniences to make our lives easier, yet computers, copiers and faxes have increased the pace of our workload rather than shortened it. And what did we do before cell phones? It seems like there are one hundred interruptions every day!

In our hurry-up world we want everything *now!* One hour dry-cleaning, instant banking and 30-second microwave dinners.

Unfortunately, our culture judges a person's worth based on the number of hours he or she works each week. It seems the *busier* you are, the more important you become.

I can remember the days when major department stores were closed on Sunday. That's a thing of the past. Now, it's one of the most profitable days of the week. When cash registers go "Ka-ching! Ka-ching!" the Lord's Day takes a back seat.

Hold on a moment! Is this what God intended when He gave Moses the Fourth Commandment? Let's take a close look:

> *Remember the Sabbath day by keeping it holy. Six days you shall labor and do all your work, but the seventh day is a Sabbath to the Lord your God. On it you shall not do any work, neither you, nor your son or daughter, nor your manservant or maidservant, nor your animals, nor the alien within your gates. For in six days the Lord made the heavens and the earth, the sea, and all that is in them, but he rested on the seventh day. Therefore the Lord blessed the Sabbath day and made it holy.*
> EXODUS 20:8-11

This is not merely a suggestion by the Almighty – it is an order!

God demands that we put into practice the principle He established at creation. According to scripture, *"Thus the heavens and the earth were completed in all their vast array. By the seventh day God had finished the work he had been doing; so on the seventh day he rested from all his work. And God blessed the seventh day and made it holy, because on it he rested from all the work of creating that he had done"* (Genesis 2:1-3).

Notice that the Creator didn't prescribe a six-day week and then begin again the next morning because His work was finished. No. He called a week *seven* days, including a 24-hour period for resting.

Since the Bible says God *"will neither slumber nor sleep"* (Psalms 121:4), He certainly didn't *need* to rest. I believe the Lord simply stopped because His work was completed. However, God also knew in advance that you and I needed an example of how to use our time.

The command to "keep the Sabbath holy" is not about whether Saturday or Sunday is the correct Lord's Day. According to the Old Testament, the Jewish people celebrate the Sabbath on Saturday. As Christians, however, we set aside Sunday – the first day of the week – to commemorate Christ's resurrection from the dead.

What's important is that we reserve a day devoted

> *The command to "keep the Sabbath holy" is not about whether Saturday or Sunday is the Lord's Day.*

totally to the Lord – to stop what we are doing and reflect on His goodness.

## Redeem the Time!

According to recent research, the average American spends over 24 hours each week watching television. It has become a convenient baby-sitter for children and an escape for adults.

I believe it's time to reclaim those hours.

You may question, "How can we win back wasted hours by stopping and resting?"

The Bible says: *"See then that ye walk circumspectly, not as fools, but as wise, redeeming the time, because the days are evil"* (Ephesians 5:15-16 KJV).

What does this mean? There's a note next to that verse in Finis Dake's *Annotated Version of the Bible*. He writes: "Redeeming the time means buying up those moments which others throw away."

Benjamin Franklin once said, "Time is money." It is also priceless – that's why we must assign it a high value.

Why is giving the Lord a special day so vital that it would be included in the Ten Commandments? Here are four reasons:

## 1. The Sabbath reminds us that God is holy.

This is the one day of creation the Lord blessed and consecrated. The word *holy* means "free from sin and sinful affections" – perfectly pure and complete in moral character.

When God blessed the Sabbath, He was saying, "I am giving you a day to step out of the cares of this imperfect life to walk into My purity – to wash yourself from an evil world and be holy, for I am holy."

This is when we redeem the lost hours of our week; to buy back those moments other people squander. Go ahead! Put the sound of your boss's voice screaming curse words out of your head for just 24 hours. Let go of the rejection you felt when a close friend turned his or her back on you.

Enter into the presence of a holy God and hear Him say: "I love you! You are Mine! Put your hand in My hand! I know where the future is leading! When others desert you, you'll feel My warm arms of compassion."

## 2. The Sabbath gives us a chance to reflect on our life.

I recently asked a woman who was walking into our church one evening, "How are you doing?"

"I need to sit down, pastor," she complained. "I'm worn out!"

*"I need to sit down, pastor," she complained. "I'm worn out!"*

Life's tendency is to press us to the max, causing us to burn the candle at both ends. As a result, we are not *winning* time, but losing it! We become exhausted – and any extra money we gain

51

slips through our tired fingers.

Stop racing through life! Devote a specific time to the Lord. Jesus says: *"Come to me, all you who are weary and burdened, and I will give you rest. Take my yoke upon you and learn from me, for I am gentle and humble in heart, and you will find rest for your souls. For my yoke is easy and my burden is light"* (Matthew 11:28-30).

*"Who am I? Why am I here? Where am I going?"*

Use every Sabbath to examine your life. "Who am I? Why am I here? Where am I going? What am I doing for God's Kingdom?"

## 3. The Sabbath directs our thoughts to the Lord.

If you spend seven days a week dwelling on your daily grind, you'll find yourself on a nerve-wrecking, never-ending downward spiral.

Sunday is when you can stop that vicious cycle by pausing, praising and worshiping the Great Jehovah. Suddenly, you are not worried and consumed with:

- "How will I get enough money to pay the bills?"
- "Will I be able to pass my school exam?"
- "Why did my parents get a divorce?"
- "Will I have a job on Monday?"

My heart goes out to those who never carve out a minute – let alone a day – for the Lord. Many become hopeless, crying, "Where's the alcohol?" "Where's the cocaine?" Even worse, "Where's the gun!"

What a glorious difference for a man or woman who walks into a house of God and feels the powerful anointing of the Holy Spirit. There is no substitute for turning your eyes, your heart, and your thoughts toward the Lord.

Like David, you will say, *"He makes me lie down in green pastures, he leads me beside quiet waters, he restores my soul"* (Psalms 23:2-3).

## 4. The Sabbath is a day of joy!

Even though I am a minister, I don't look at Sunday as a "work day." Quite the reverse. It is a time to rejoice – to celebrate.

I rise at the crack of dawn, shower, get dressed and head to my desk to look over the message I'm going to deliver. In my heart I'm excited and say "Thank You Lord. This is Your day!"

Arriving at the church early, I meet with other pastors on our staff and we begin praying for the services – even walking through the sanctuary and laying our hands on every chair. "Lord," I pray, "when people sit here may they feel the power of the Holy Spirit!"

We walk up and down the aisles, praying for the beauty of Christ to fill the auditorium. Then, before long, the cars begin to roll in and fill the parking lot, the lights come on, the choir is singing and we are praising His name.

It's Sunday. The most joyful day of my week!

## TIME FOR GOD – TIME FOR FAMILY

We live in a Jewish neighborhood, and it's amazing to watch our neighbors on Friday evenings as their "Shabbat" begins. It seems like every driveway at each house is jammed with cars. On Saturdays we often see individual families walking down the streets, mother, father and children, talking, discussing the Sabbath.

Many still hold to the custom of not driving their cars on Saturday. They choose to walk as a way of honoring God.

In the home where my sisters and I were raised, Sundays were set aside totally for the Lord. The routine never changed. It was church, dinner, a nap, and back for the evening service.

As an eight-year-old, that Sunday nap was the most troubling event of my week. At 3:30 in the afternoon, I'd try everything imaginable to get to sleep – but it rarely worked. When we were a little older, my parents let us burn off energy by playing outside – as long as we weren't too rambunctious!

What a treasured memory of being together as a family and honoring God on His day.

## Sundays with our Sons

Our first year in Miami was probably the most difficult year I've ever experienced in my life. My wife and I had been married for about 25 years, but you must realize the previous almost 18 years we had lived right next door to her parents in Tacoma, Washington. Every week I boarded a plane on Saturday and flew somewhere in the world to minister, usually arriving back home on Thursday.

For eighteen years, including 1,600,000 air miles, I traveled and preached the gospel. We had our family – plus our extended family – in-laws, aunts, uncles, cousins.

When our oldest son was approaching eighteen, during his senior year in high school, we followed God's call to come to Miami – leaving behind everything that was familiar and secure. We were now  with people we were just learning to know and love. The weeks were hectic, but Sunday afternoons we reserved specifically for our family. And, as lonely as we were for those back home on the West Coast, we were drawn together in an unusually tight bond we had never before experienced as a family – just the six of us. My wife and I, plus Jonfulton, Richie, Taylor and Graham

*"Come on," I would say. "Let's go for a walk."*

Oh, how we looked forward to those Sunday

afternoons – a great meal, a walk on the beach, and playing a little touch football. Then the week would start again.

I vividly remember that first year. More than once, late in the evening, I would walk by the room of one of our sons and see his head buried in a pillow, quietly crying, missing his buddies back home. "Come on," I would say, "Let's go for a walk."

We would drive to the beach we loved and talk about the greatness of God – and how He is holding our lives in His hands, and has our future charted.

Before long the sorrow would pass and the joy would return. We were ready to face another day.

**"It's Going to be Okay!"**

It was a Friday morning at the end of August – a time I had not been looking forward to. Our oldest son, Jonfulton, was leaving to go away to university. You know it's going to happen, yet you are never quite prepared.

I glanced in his room about 10 o'clock in the morning. He was to leave a few hours later. The room was unusually clean – somewhat alarming! His bags were packed and he was sitting on the bed, reading.

I looked at him and said, "Son?"

"Hi, Dad, what's wrong?"

"Why don't the two of us go to the beach for a walk?" I asked.

He looked at me rather puzzled and said, "Dad, I'm just

fine. There's no problem at all."

With a lump in my throat, I admitted, "We're not going there for you. This time it's for me."

"Oh, okay, Dad."

We climbed in the car and drove down to the beach together.

I'll never forget it. We stood by the water's edge and the Atlantic was like a lake that day – hardly a ripple. Jonfulton is quite tall, about 6'3". He put his arm over my shoulder and I put my arm around his waist. Tears were streaming down my cheeks.

"Son," I began, "you know the Bible says that if you'll cast your bread upon the waters, one day it will come back to you. This afternoon your mother and I will take you to the airport, and we will cast you into God's divine providence. We believe that one day, perhaps with a wife, maybe with several children, we don't know – He will bring you back to us."

Jonfulton put his arm around me, saying, "Dad, it's going to be okay."

On the beach that had become our Sunday afternoon sanctuary, instead of me encouraging and praying for him, my son prayed for me.

**What does Sunday mean to you?**

Remembering the Sabbath and keeping it holy is not a judgment, rather a privilege and a joy. Make it what the Lord intends – a time to worship, a time to praise, a time for your family to celebrate the goodness of God and find a greater intimacy with Him.

DECISIONS

*How do you let God know His Day is special?*

*What personal benefits do you receive by keeping the Sabbath holy?*

*Specifically, what steps will you take to make Sunday more meaningful to you and your family?*

# HONORING YOUR ELDERS ADDS YEARS TO YOUR LIFE

*The child who never learns to obey his parents in*
*the home will not obey God or man outside of the home.*
— SUSANNE WESLEY

It is tragic to see cracks appearing in what was once the foundation of America's strength. I'm talking about strong, loving families – from the poor to the wealthy, and every home in between.

It wasn't long ago that the average child in our nation had two parents and four grandparents. Today, it's often much more complicated. Far too often I hear young people explain: "He's my biological father," or "my birth

59

parent." "She's my mom – but really she is my step mom." One ten-year-old told me: "I call her mom because I don't have a mom – she's really my grandmother."

Yet, centuries ago, God established a law we cannot ignore. The Fifth Commandment states:

> *Honor your father and your mother, so that you*
> *may live long in the land the Lord your God is giving you.*
> EXODUS 20:12

It's a command that includes a promise. The Lord says, "If you obey what I am telling you, you will enjoy a long life."

However, the future some people envision is far different. I've read bumper stickers with these words: BE NICE TO YOUR CHILDREN. THEY'RE THE ONES WHO WILL CHOOSE YOUR NURSING HOME, or HONOR THY FATHER AND THY MOTHER – FOR THEY HAVEN'T YET WRITTEN THEIR WILL.

We may laugh at those statements, but they are often more real than we'd like to admit.

## It Starts with Mom and Dad

Before we examine the issue of esteeming our parents, there are a few vital things every mom and dad needs to know concerning raising their *own* children. How can they be trained to bestow such an honor?

If you want to see virtue and character established in

your sons and daughters, here are three principles worth practicing:

**First: Raise the moral fences in your home.**

Fixed boundaries and parameters for your children are absolutely essential. The fences confirm: "You are safe in this area!" It lets them know how far they can go.

The precept is nothing new. God gave Adam and Eve a huge boundary to live within, and there was only one rule. A certain tree – called "The Tree of the Knowledge of Good and Evil" – was off limits.

We all know what happened when they disobeyed. Not only did they lose all their privileges, they allowed sin to enter into mankind.

Parents, you have an obligation to set godly standards for your children to adhere to.

*Fixed boundaries and parameters for your children are absolutely essential.*

As an eight-year-old I can remember my mother sternly warning me: "I don't want that neighbor boy coming over to this house. I don't like what he represents!"

At first I wondered, "Well, what in the world does my buddy *represent?*"

However, my parents knew best. It was in the middle of summer and we didn't have air-conditioning. And every night we would hear my friend's mother and father fighting. They would constantly get drunk and start screaming and throwing things at each other.

It wasn't the son who was involved, but my parents didn't want that spirit brought into our home. So they raised a fence to protect me.

As I became older, they extended and even lowered some of the fences when they felt I could take personal responsibility for my actions and associates.

Robyn and I have raised our sons in the same way. Of course, each child thinks the rules are too light for their younger siblings. My oldest, Jonfulton, said about his brother Rich, "Dad, you've got no rules for him at all. You used to stand over me with hand grenades. Why not treat him the same way?"

*Without rules and standards you will raise rudderless children who are incapable of making moral choices.*

Well, that's also what Rich says about Graham – who feels the same about Taylor. Yet, as parents we are totally aware of the boundaries we establish for each child.

If you are familiar with sail boats and ships, you understand it is the rudder that gives the direction in the middle of a storm. So it is with our sons and daughters. Without rules and standards you will raise *rudderless* children who are incapable of making moral choices – who will flounder or capsize in a crisis.

Read what God states concerning this issue: *"Fix these*

*words of mine in your hearts and minds; tie them as symbols on your hands and bind them on your foreheads. Teach them to your children, talking about them when you sit at home and when you walk along the road, when you lie down and when you get up"* (Deuteronomy 11:18-19).

The Lord is saying: "Erect those fences! Teach your children morality!"


**Second: Practice what you preach!**

Setting rules and boundaries mean absolutely nothing to your children if you don't live by them yourself. You can't teach the commandments by breaking them on a regular basis. For example, if you use foul language it's impossible to tell your son or daughter *not* to!

I pray because my father prays! I do my best to live a godly life because my parents do. In the Hebrew tradition, the word for *parent* is related to the word for *teacher*. Jewish people have always believed that parents are teachers of faith and morality.

The only way to instill truth into the hearts and minds of your children is to model it through your daily living.

Some parents shirk that responsibility by rationalizing, "We'll just enroll him in a Christian school. I am sure they will teach him well." Or, "If we take her to Sunday School, I know she'll learn right from wrong!"

At best, Christian schools and churches can only reinforce what is being taught within the walls of your home. That's where instruction begins.

As a pastor, I can tell you that we can only facilitate your words and actions. If children aren't spiritually grounded at home, we are up against incredible obstacles.

Solomon was the wisest and richest king who ever lived. Why? Because he had a good role model for a father. Even when David had a moral failure, he did the right thing by repenting – maintaining what God saw in him: *"a man after his own heart"* (1 Samuel 13:14).

Listen to what Solomon said to the Lord: *"You have shown great kindness to David my father and have made me king in his place. Now, Lord God, let your promise to my father David be confirmed, for you have made me king over a people who are as numerous as the dust of the earth. Give me wisdom and knowledge, that I may lead this people, for who is able to govern this great people of yours?"* (2 Chronicles 1:8-10).

Solomon honored both his earthly and Heavenly Father – and God in turn honored him.

Remember, practice what you preach!

**Third: Let your children know you love them.**

Every child needs to hear the words, "I love you," and to see love demonstrated.

For some reason, those three words are so difficult for many fathers to say. They'll call a son into the room and begin, "Son, have a seat."

"What is it, Dad?"

"I just wanted to say something that I've been thinking about and want to tell you today," the dad begins. "It's important to me that you know this!"

"Okay, go ahead and tell me," the son responds.

"Well, the father mumbles, "I just want to tell you that I looo... Ah! Son, I looo... You're a good kid. Go on now, and have a great day!"

The dad just couldn't bring himself to say the words, "I love you!"

That's not true of the Wilkerson home. From the beginning, we followed the biblical principle: *"Train up a child in the way he should go; and when he is old, he will not depart from it"* (Proverbs 22:6 KJV).

*I threw the ball and asked them to throw it back. It was training time!*

When the boys were little, I didn't just say, "I love you." I'd add. "Now say it back to me!" And they would repeat, "I love you too."

I threw the ball and asked them to throw it back. It was *training* time!

Even now, our phone conversations end with: "I love you, son."

"I love you, too, Dad."

God Himself established this principle. His Son, Jesus, was at the river of Jordan, being baptized by His cousin John. As He came up out of the water, the Father was so happy – so in love with His Son – that the Bible records

God ripped the heavens open and released a dove (Mark 1:10).

Then, the Father announces these words so that everyone in the vicinity could hear them: *"You are my Son, whom I love; with you I am well pleased"* (v.11).

Yes, God told Jesus, "I love You, Son!"

How about your relationship with your son or daughter? Early in their life you must set the stage for good things to happen in the future. This is accomplished by prayerfully raising the fences, practicing what you preach and continually letting your children know how much you love them.

## IT's A TWO-WAY STREET

Much sooner than you realize, the shoe is on the other foot. Instead of parents training their children, it's time for sons and daughters to begin honoring their parents.

I've heard children of all ages grumble, "My parents treat me like a kid!"

Well, to them you are, and always will be! There once was a day when you were not a parent, but now that you are, there'll never be a day you aren't!

It's amazing how parents have difficulty accepting their children as adults. I laughed when I heard a 90-year-old comment about her 70-year old daughter, "That girl of mine doesn't have a brain in her head!"

Of course, that "girl" was already a great-grandmother.

As a parent, that's always going to be your child – and it is difficult for moms and dads to let go.

When you complain, "My parents treat me like a kid," you are really saying, "They don't respect me or value my opinion!"

The street named Honor and Respect runs two ways, and needs to be walked by both mothers, fathers and children.

## How can dishonorable parents be respected?

As a child, you are under orders from God Himself to honor your father and your mother.

Confused, you may say, "Rich, you don't understand what I've gone through with my parents! They've given me Hell!"

One man, with tears streaming down his cheeks, cried, "How can I respect my parents when they abused me as a child and then ran out on me?"

We have to face reality. There are a growing number of people who have suffered both psychological and physical abuse at the hands of their parents. Sadly, the scars run deep.

*"How can I respect my parents when they abused me as a child and then ran out on me?"*

Perhaps you are one of those individuals, and wonder how you can keep the Fifth Commandment when you know how you were mistreated.

I sincerely believe that as a child of abuse, it is your responsibility to break the *cycle* of abuse. It starts with forgiving the parent who showed such disrespect, asking God for inner healing, then reaching out to the offender with the love that only Christ can give.

There is no alternative to God's commandments. Let me suggest that you add one more word and say: "Honor your father and your mother *anyway!*"

**Your broken lineage can be restored.**

Just because your family tree is contaminated, doesn't mean the fruit will always remain bitter.

One of the most despicable rulers to ever lead Israel was the son of Hezekiah – King Manasseh. During his 55-year reign he built altars to Baal, practiced sorcery and *"did much evil in the eyes of the Lord"* (2 Kings 21:11). The Bible says he *"shed so much innocent blood that he filled Jerusalem from end to end"* (v.16.).

> *Just because your family tree is contaminated, doesn't mean the fruit will always remain bitter.*

What a lousy king – and his son, Amon, wasn't much better. Once more, Israel had an evil leader who *"walked in the ways of his father; he worshiped the idols his father had worshiped"* (v.21).

After two years, the people conspired against Amon and assassinated him in the palace. Taking his place was

Amon's eight-year-old son, Josiah.

Talk about a 180-degree turn! Read what scripture says about this young man: *"He did what was right in the eyes of the Lord and walked in all the ways of his father David, not turning aside to the right or to the left"* (2 Kings 22:2).

You may say, "I thought Josiah was the son of Amon." That is true, but his role model was David – his father long removed. If you read the "begats" in Matthew 1 you'll find that David was in Josiah's lineage 13 generations earlier.

How does a young man with such horrendous breeding ascend to the throne and do the right thing? And why did he decide to emulate David?

**Choose a new pattern for your life.**

We don't know much about Josiah's mother, Jedidah, or his grandmother, but they must have been incredibly good women. I say that because moms make it happen! Someone knew the Lord and trained that boy in the way he should go.

When Josiah reached the age where he learned about his father and grandfather, he obviously made some choices. Would he follow in their corrupt footsteps, or listen to his mother's training to be a man of God?

I believe this young man began to trace his lineage as far back as he could – and read the psalms of David. I can hear Josiah exclaiming, "Now there's someone I can connect with – a man I can pattern my life after."

That's exactly what Josiah did as he *"turned to the Lord...with all his heart and with all his soul and with all his strength"* (2 Kings 23:25-26).

Because of his actions – by breaking the curse – he actually honored his father by restoring the throne of Israel to what the Lord intended.

**Establish a heritage worth passing on.**

If you have undgodly people in your background, follow Josiah's example. Go back to an individual in your heritage who was a man or woman of God and choose that person as a role model for your life. It may be a grandfather, or an aunt, who was full of the Holy Spirit. Declare, "That's how I am going to live!"

In the process, you'll be able to honor your father and mother by starting a new lineage. Your children – and your children's children – will look back and remember daddy or grandmother with joy and gladness.

Friend, it is the will of God to even give honor to a person who abused you. When you do, by the Grace of the Father, the chain of pain is going to break. You will not pass this burden down to your children.

I'm sure at one time or another you've told someone: "What goes around comes around." Are you living out that phrase in your own life? Remember, if you honor your parents, your children will be taught to love, respect and obey. In the process you, too, will be blessed.

Receive the words of King David: *"Blessed are all who fear the Lord who walk in his ways. You will eat the fruit of your labor; blessings and prosperity will be yours. Your wife will be like a fruitful vine within your house; your sons will be like olive shoots around your table. Thus is the man blessed who fears the Lord. May the Lord bless you from Zion all the days of your life; may you see the prosperity of Jerusalem, and may you live to see your children's children"* (Psalms 128:1-6).

What a heritage for your family!

## DECISIONS

*In what ways (now or in the past)
have you let your parents know
that you honor them?*

*What changes would you make to earn
more respect from your children?*

*Name the creative way you can tell
your mom or dad, "I love you."*

# YOU CELEBRATE LIFE BY YOUR ACTIONS!

*Take my hand – not my life!*

– A BUMPER STICKER

T he phone rang late one Saturday night. It was Clyde Preston, one of the ministers on our staff.

"Pastor," he began, "I have some very bad news."

"What is it?" I wanted to know.

"Today, one of the ladies of our church was shot by her husband who wasn't a Christian. Then he turned the gun on himself and he is also dead. They just found the bodies."

With a trembling voice, Clyde continued, "Pastor, they have one daughter, a 12-year old girl. This weekend she has been staying with friends from the church and doesn't know what has taken place." Then he added, "We need to pray because tomorrow between services, we're going to have to tell this little girl what happened."

I had only been the pastor of Trinity Church for a few weeks and this would be my first funeral to officiate in Miami.

Four days later there were two caskets resting at the front of our sanctuary. The family of this fallen women were believers and insisted it be a joint funeral because they wanted the husband's family – who were not Christians – to know that forgiveness is possible through Jesus Christ our Lord.

That morning after I preached the funeral message, I watched as this precious daughter who had been raised up in our children's ministry stood between the two caskets. She placed one hand on her mother's chest and the other hand on her father. Then, crying, she screamed: "I have no Mommy and I have no Daddy!"

It was a heart-wrenching experience. And I kept thinking to myself "Why do people refuse to listen? Why do they foolishly ignore God's rules for life?"

The Sixth Commandment declares:

*You shall not murder.*
EXODUS 20:13

## THE ULTIMATE PENALTY

There was a time in American history when murder was an unusual occurrence, but not today. It has become commonplace. Just flip on the six-o'clock news and you'll see another cloth-draped body being wheeled to an ambulance. In the past 12 months over 23,000 individuals were murdered in this country. And without the rapid response of modern medicine, experts say that figure would have escalated to over 65,000.

What does God say about those who commit murder? The Bible declares that if you take the life of another human being, your life should also be taken: *"Whoever sheds the blood of man, by man shall his blood be shed; for in the image of God has God made man"* (Genesis 9:6).

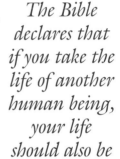

*The Bible declares that if you take the life of another human being, your life should also be taken.*

That same biblical law has found its way into our judicial system. Today, however, we categorize various levels of punishment for those guilty of homicide. The ultimate penalty is reserved for those who commit cold-blooded, premeditated murder. This is for the person who plots and schemes – then sticks a gun in a victim's chest and callously pulls the trigger. For that crime you will face a maximum sentence.

Thirty-eight states have the death penalty – or capital punishment – on their statute books.

There are also crimes of passion. For example, a husband or wife arrives home to unexpectedly find a spouse committing adultery. Suddenly, consumed with rage, a life is tragically taken. In such an instance, the punishment is usually much less than for the person committing premeditated murder.

Let's examine another level of homicide. Two people begin to fight over some trivial matter. Then, accidently, one of them falls to the ground and hits their head on a sharp object and dies. This is a form of murder, even though it wasn't calculated in advance.

Regardless of the degree of punishment, every murder is an attack on God Almighty.

## Life is sacred to the Lord.

If you study scripture, you'll find the emphasis is on *celebrating life* – not extinguishing it. God declares: "*Do not seek revenge or bear a grudge against one of your people, but love your neighbor as yourself. I am the Lord*" (Leviticus 19:18).

*From the beginning, the Creator has been concerned with life, not death.*

"Getting even" with someone is not our responsibility, but God's. He declares, "*Vengeance is mine; I will repay, saith the Lord*" (Romans 12:19 KJV).

From the beginning, the Creator has been concerned with life, not death. The Lord formed man "*from the dust of the ground and breathed into his nostrils the breath of life, and the man became a living being*" (Genesis 2:7).

You and I are much more than well-developed protoplasm. We are eternal beings – with the breath of

God providing oxygen to our blood at this very moment. As the Word tells us, *"the life of every creature is its blood"* (Leviticus 17:14). Without God's divine breath we would perish.

This is crucial because when a person ends the life of another – whether in a fit of rage, or cool, calm and collected – they are actually stealing the very breath of God from that individual.

Can you see the consequences? A murderer will have to answer to more than the police or a jury. God Himself has been offended. That is why He says, "Since you have taken one of My precious lives, I demand your life in return."

## There is a significant difference between murder and killing.

The Old Testament is filled with examples of God's hatred of evil – often resulting in the death of His enemies. Don't forget what happened to Sodom and Gomorrah? Scripture records that *"the smoke of the country went up as the smoke of a furnace. And it came to pass [that] God destroyed the cities of the plain"* (Genesis 19:28-29).

Today, we have hundreds of thousands of young men and women serving in the Armed Forces. Many will be called upon to defend freedom by taking the life of a terrorist or an enemy combatant. In the eyes of the law, this is not considered murder, rather an act to protect our nation.

Remember, the Lord instructs us to: *"Obey your leaders*

*and submit to their authority"* (Hebrews 13:17).

## What About Suicide?

As a minister, I have often been asked, 'Is suicide murder?" And the follow-up question is usually, "Did the person go to heaven or hell?"

Suicide claims the lives of nearly 30,000 annually in the United States. Even more alarming, research reveals that an estimated five million living Americans have *attempted* suicide.

Taken at face value, it's easy to say, "Of course suicide is murder – after all, by premeditation a life has been taken." But what does the Bible say?

There is a scripture in Revelation that lists eight categories of people who are headed for hell: *"...the cowardly, the unbelieving, the vile, the murderers, the sexually immoral, those who practice magic arts, the idolaters and all liars – their place will be in the fiery lake"* (Revelation 21:8).

However, there is a qualification. Such people will spend eternity in hell *unless* they get right with God – and that includes murderers. The Word declares, *"For whosoever shall call upon the name of the Lord shall be saved"* (Romans 10:13 KJV). We are all destined for eternal punishment until we ask Jesus to forgive us and allow Him to set us on the right path.

God knows us better than we know ourselves. The Bible says, *"You are not your own; you were bought at a price"* (1 Corinthians 6:19-20). The payment was the blood Christ shed at Calvary.

Personally, I believe God's grace is extended to every born again believer – even one who, for whatever reason, takes his own life.

Who are we to judge what lies in the heart of a man or woman?

## 1. The Lord's mercy is beyond our understanding.

I'm glad you and I are not God. If we were, hell would probably have a population explosion!

We see someone make a mistake and piously exclaim, "That's wrong. He's living in sin and is headed for eternity with the devil!"

*Who are we to judge what is in the heart of a man or woman?*

Our Lord, however, is a God of overwhelming grace and compassion. His mercy is indescribable. If you were judged on your thought patterns for the past twenty-four hours, what would God say concerning you? How about your dreams? Would you like them to be projected on a screen for the world to see?

The fact that any of us are alive is a testament to the marvelous mercy of our loving Lord.

## 2. God offers us a way of escape.

There's no need to take matters into your own hands, when your Heavenly Father is waiting to provide you with help and hope. As the apostle Paul writes: *"No temptation has seized you except what is common to man. And God is faithful; he will not let you be tempted beyond what you can bear. But when you are tempted, he will also provide a way out so that you can stand up under it*" (1 Corinthians 10:13).

Turn your anxiety and cares over to the Giver of Life.

## THE ISSUE OF ABORTION

Since the 1973 Supreme Court decision in *Roe v. Wade* making it legal, there has been an epidemic of abortions in our nation. Yet the question remains: Is abortion murder?

*Is abortion murder? According to God's Word, the answer is an unequivocal "yes!"*

According to God's Word, the answer is an unequivocal "yes!" It is the taking of a life.

Consider this biblical example: "*If men who are fighting hit a pregnant woman and she gives birth prematurely but there is no serious injury, the offender must be fined whatever the woman's husband demands and the court allows. But if there is serious injury, you are to take life for life*" (Exodus 21:22-23).

In other words, God says if a man is fighting with a woman, and because of that physical confrontation, the woman miscarries and the baby dies, the man's life should be taken for repayment.

If God makes such a judgment on a miscarriage, what must He think when it comes to abortion? – when a woman intentionally goes to a doctor to have her baby destroyed.

Most men think they never have to deal with the issue of abortion. Yet, when a woman chooses this procedure, whoever impregnated her will be equally accountable when he stands before God.

Perhaps someone reading this book has made the choice at some point to have an abortion. Rather than judge you, allow me to give you two *hopes* on the subject:

**Hope #1: That child is now with the Lord.**

God does not punish children to a death sentence because of the actions of their parents – even if that life was taken while still in the womb. You can rest assured your unborn child is now with the Lord and you will see that baby again!

**Hope #2: You can be forgiven for your actions.**

Earlier in my ministry I was speaking in a large church in London, Ontario. My message that Sunday morning was on "Private Pain" – the kinds of anguish we suffer alone.

I touched on the issue of abortion and made the statement, "My friend, you can be forgiven. God can take you to a higher place and let you know what you did is under His precious blood."

As I concluded the message, I asked those who were struggling with private pain to come forward. The altars were quickly jammed with several hundred people.

Up in the balcony to my left, I heard a woman begin to weep. She was loudly sobbing – and then a joyous laughter came over her. Several ushers tried to calm her while I focused my attention on the altar service.

When the meeting was over and people were leaving, the woman who was in the balcony came up to me and said, "Reverend Wilkerson, I want you to know this morning my life has been changed."

She began, "You spoke about abortion and I had one about 20 years ago. I was part of the Hippy Movement then and all the people at my university were into free love. We felt like anything we did only had implications on our own life and no one else. 'Live and let live' was our motto."

> *"We felt like anything we did only had implications for our own life and no one else."*

I quietly listened as she poured out her heart. "Many of my girlfriends had babies out of wedlock, and others abortions – some had more than one," she recalled.

"I had an abortion." She explained how she was into situational ethics and was just following through on her philosophy of life. "But when my baby was taken from me through abortion, even as an unbeliever, I was a miserable, broken person. From that day forward, never a day went by when I didn't think about it  – all day long."

Now, with tears welling up in her eyes, she said, "Over fifteen years ago, I accepted Jesus Christ as my personal Savior, and my sins were forgiven. I met a wonderful man of God and we married. We have three children who are all in a Christian school and are being raised to serve the Lord."

The woman told me how much she loves God and never misses church. The she added, rather ashamed, "But even as a Christian the thought of what I did 20 years ago still haunts me. Every day I hear the devil whisper, 'You murdered your baby!'"

She explained, "Sometimes I'm able to go just so far in God, and then a guilt trip overwhelms me. I think to myself, 'There's no hope.'"

With a broad smile changing her countenance, the woman continued, "But this morning, while you were praying for us at the altar, I was standing up in the balcony feeling guilty like I had a million times before. All of a sudden, with my hands raised, I looked up into the dome of this sanctuary, and to my amazement, I saw Jesus Christ hovering above the crowd. His eyes looked straight into mine, and He was holding my baby in His hands."

She continued, "Jesus looked into my face and said, 'I have your child. Your baby's fine. Let this be under My blood. It's time to get on with the rest of your life.'"

Now, with a heart of joy, she exclaimed, "This morning, pastor, something broke in the spirit world, and I was set completely free! Finally, there is freedom in my life."

Oh, the liberation that comes from the Lord!

## IS "MERCY KILLING" JUSTIFIED?
Thank God, Dr. Jack Kevorkian is behind bars. The

man who helped at least 130 people take their own lives was sentenced in 1999 to between 10 and 25 years.

Some call euthanasia – ending the life of the old or terminally ill – "death by dignity." I call it murder.

I would hate to stand before the Lord as a serial killer who purposely took the lives of dozens of sick, elderly patients.

The problem with euthanasia and abortion is the same. We are killing those who cannot speak for themselves. It takes us down a road that eventually can lead to mass extermination. Never forget the Holocaust. Adolph Hitler and the Nazi government passed laws that made possible the killing of six million innocent Jews.

We simply cannot play God. He alone is the One who determines the length of our lives. *"In his hand is the life of every creature and the breath of all mankind"* (Job 12:10).

## MURDERING WITH YOUR TONGUE

There is also a method of killing seldom linked with murder, yet the results are often as devastating. It involves tale-bearing and slander.

Gossip is a killer. It destroys people's character and kills their reputation. In the Hebrew tradition, humiliating someone publically or talking behind their back was related to the sin of murder.

The Bible places a high priority on our words. *"The tongue has the power of life and death"* (Proverbs 18:21). What is released from your mouth must uplift and edify, not demean and destroy.

Scripture warns: *"Do not go about spreading slander among your people"* (Leviticus 19:16). Why? Because gossip has serious consequences. The second part of this verse reads: *"Do not do anything that endangers your neighbor's life."*

Whew! That's a serious matter!

Don't ignore the story of Miriam, the sister of Moses. This woman, who was once called a *"prophetess"* (Exodus 15:20) was stricken in the Old Testament with leprosy for gossiping against the man of God (Numbers 12:1-13).

**The damage caused by words is permanent.**

I heard about a man who spoke evil of his Rabbi. Convicted of his wayward tongue, he went to the cleric and confessed his sin. Then he asked the Rabbi, "Is there something I can do to make penance?"

*"Is there something I can do to make penance?"*

The Rabbi thought for a moment and said, "Here, I want you to take this feather pillow to the top of that hill over there. Then cut it open and release all the feathers out of the pillowcase."

Gladly, the man followed the Rabbi's orders. He raced up the hill and cut open the pillow. The wind caught the thousands of feathers and they fluttered and blew all over the valley. They became lodged everywhere – in the trees, bushes and grass. The man returned smiling. "I did what you told me!" he joyfully exclaimed.

The Rabi, however, wasn't finished. To the astonished man, he said "Let me complete your penance. Now I want you to take the pillow case back to the mountain, and don't return until you have gathered every one of the feathers and put them back into the pillow case.

The man stared in disbelief. His face fell. "But Rabbi" he said, "How can I? That would be impossible!"

The Rabbi nodded and responded, "That's the problem with gossip. It travels so fast. It crosses the water before noon. It goes over the airways – through phone lines and cell towers. It's everywhere, and you can never totally repair the harm you have caused.

**People gossip to raise their own status by putting someone else down.**

Belittling a friend is a telltale sign of poor self-esteem. If you are going to find fault with someone, make certain that person is yourself!

And something else: the person who listens to gossip is just as guilty as the one who spreads it.

If you love to hear harmful tales about others, it may be because you are battling evil yourself. King Solomon wrote: *"A wicked man listens to evil lips; a liar pays attention to a malicious tongue"* (Proverbs 17:4).

Listen to these words written by an anonymous author:

*My name is gossip.*
*I have no respect for justice*
*I maim without killing.*
*I break hearts and ruin lives*
*I am cunning and malicious and gather strength with*
*    age.*
*The more I am quoted, the more I am believed.*
*I flourish at every level of society.*
*My victims are helpless.*
*They cannot protect themselves against me.*
*Because I have no face, to track me down is impossible.*
*The harder you try, the more elusive I become.*
*I am nobody's friend.*
*Once I tarnish a reputation, it is never the same.*
*I topple governments, wreck marriages and ruin*
*    careers.*
*I cause sleepless nights, heartaches, and indigestion.*
*I spawn suspicion and generate grief.*
*I make innocent people cry in their pillows.*
*Even my name hisses.*
*I make headlines and headaches.*
*Before you repeat a story, ask yourself, "Is it true? Is it*
*    fair? Is it necessary?"*
*If not, shut up!*

Killing with words is not what God intends. When Jesus walked the earth He declared: *"The thief cometh not, but for to steal, and to kill, and to destroy: I am come that they might have life, and that they might have it more abundantly"* (John 10:10 KJV).

Friend, everything murder represents is the exact opposite of what the kingdom of heaven is built upon. Satan spreads fear, destruction and death while God inspires us with His faith and hope and the promise of eternity with Him.

The Lord is asking you to *"choose life"* (Deuteronomy 30:19). Your future depends on your decision.

### DECISIONS

*Other than by physical means, how do people harm others?*

*Why should judgment be placed in God's hands instead of ours?*

*According to Scripture, what does the Lord say about forgiveness?*

# THE BOND OF MARRIAGE MUST REMAIN UNBROKEN

*It is better not to vow than
to make a vow and not fulfill it.*

−ECCLESIASTES 5:5

In jest, a man told the story of Moses coming down from the mountain with two tablets in his hands. As the people gathered around him, Moses announced, "I have some good news and some bad news! The good news is that I got Him to limit the commandments to ten. The bad news is that God would not throw out the one about adultery!"

Comedians and their audiences delight in poking fun at the frailty of human nature, yet it is really no laughing matter. The Seventh Commandment is a blunt statement that leaves no "wiggle room." God demands:

*You shall not commit adultery.*
EXODUS 20:14

It is obvious to me there's a widening gulf between the way we celebrate Father's Day and Mother's Day. We honor our moms with great joy and pleasure – a time much like Thanksgiving. When it comes to dads, however, it seems there is less and less emphasis each year.

Could it be because countless thousands of children across this nation don't know who their fathers are?

**Adultery is about broken promises.**

Every day, millions of men and women break their marriage vows – to their spouses, their children, and even worse, to God.

According to a recent study reported by the Associated Press, 22 percent of married men and 14 percent of the married women in the United States have had an adulterous affair. If you apply that to today's American population, 19 million men who are married have committed adultery; 12 million women who are married have done the same.

Here is what is shocking about these statistics.

THE BOND OF MARRIAGE MUST REMAIN UNBROKEN

Approximately 70 percent of wives were unaware their husbands were cheating on them. And 54 percent of husbands did not know their wife was being unfaithful. Why? Because the problem is so insidious. It is filled with secrecy and deception.

The word adultery derives from the term which means to contaminate, make impure or defile. Scripture warns: *"Moreover thou shalt not lie carnally with thy neighbour's wife, to defile thyself with her"* (Leviticus 18:20 KJV). Even more, *"a man who commits adultery lacks judgment; whoever does so destroys himself"* (Proverbs 6:32).

> ✍
> *The word adultery derives from the term which means to contaminate, make impure or defile.*

**A lesson in fidelity.**

There's an astonishing story in the Old Testament of God telling the prophet Hosea, *"Go, take to yourself an adulterous wife and children of unfaithfulness"* (Hosea 1:2).

So Hosea chose to marry Gomer, a promiscuous Israeli woman, and together they had three children.

Why would the Lord even suggest such a thing? It was *"because the land is guilty of the vilest adultery in departing from the Lord"* (v.2).

God used this relationship – the suffering of one of His prophets married to a harlot – to illustrate His own sorrow of being married to Israel. While the nation continued to whore after other deities, God's heart was broken. Through it all, Hosea remained a loyal, loving husband.

The lesson of this story is that the fidelity we have for our husband or wife usually corresponds to our faithfulness to God.

Let me put it bluntly. You cannot expect to enjoy eternity with your Heavenly Father if you are a philanderer, stepping out on your spouse. Such a life indicates that you have no true relationship with God.

You may worry, "It's too late! I've already crossed the line and cheated on my spouse."

My friend, the Lord understands your situation. The Bible tells us: *"For all have sinned and fall short of the glory of God"* (Romans 3:23).

The reason God sent His Son to die on the Cross was to remove the stain of iniquity from your life. I can tell you on the authority of God's Word if you have committed adultery you can be forgiven by the cleansing blood of Jesus.

**There's a great difference between "holy sex" and "unholy sex."**

Scripture makes the distinction.

The only sex which meets God's approval is that which takes place between a husband and wife in fulfillment of their marital relationship. *"Marriage should be honored by* all, and the marriage bed kept pure, for God will judge the adulterer and all the sexually immoral" (Hebrews 13:4).

If you were to ask me, "What is unholy sex?" I'd give you a two word answer: "Everything else!"

From the beginning, the Lord made it crystal clear He does not condone promiscuity among men or women – and that sex is ordained only for marriage.

Look at this interesting pronouncement to the children of Israel: *"If a man happens to meet a virgin who is not pledged to be married and rapes her and they are discovered, he shall pay the girl's father fifty shekels of silver. He must marry the girl, for he has violated her. He can never divorce her as long as he lives"* (Deuteronomy 22:28-29).

> *From the beginning, the Lord made it crystal clear that He does not condone promiscuity – and that sex is ordained only for marriage.*

To most people, having intimate relations with a person prior to marriage is called premarital sex. God calls it rape!

It makes no difference if you offer the excuse, "She wanted to," or "He wanted to." According to scripture they raped each other. This passage refers to both *pre* and *marital* intercourse. Sexual relations obligated a man to marry the woman.

In Jewish tradition, all non-marital sexual activity was referred to as prostitution. If you were having sex outside of marriage, you were prostituting yourself and so was your partner.

In today's pop culture it's not unusual for a young man in a club to introduce his girlfriend, "This is my ho!" – slang for whore! How debasing! The woman could also say the same thing since biblically speaking they are both prostitutes!

> We use the term "holy matrimony" because when the vows of marriage are made before God, they are consecrated unto Him.

You can be the most educated, well-dressed, prosperous businessman in town, but if you are cheating on your wife, in God's eyes it is whoredom.

**Marriage sanctifies sex.**

We use the term "holy matrimony" because when the vows of marriage are made before God, they are consecrated unto Him. From that moment forward the sexual activities of that union are sanctified.

At creation, God declared: *"It is not good for the man to be alone. I will make a helper suitable for him"* (Genesis 2:18). *"For this reason a man will leave his father and mother and be united to his wife, and they will become one flesh"* (v.24).

The Lord blessed them and said, *"Be fruitful, and*

*multiply* (Genesis 1:28 KJV).

## SMART STEPS

You may say, "Yes, I am married and know what God says, but I am also human and have needs and feelings. How can I avoid adultery?

Let me share these four vital steps:

**Step one: Stay in love with your spouse.**

Do you remember when you fell head over heels in love with the person who is now your spouse? There was electricity, desire – the need to be with each other. Such passion doesn't have to end.

Even now, relive those moments and allow the fires of love to be rekindled.

**Step two: Make the house of the Lord the center of your activities.**

Millions who confess to adultery admit, "I was in the wrong place at the wrong time." You change those odds dramatically when you attend church faithfully and surround yourself with a body of believers.

**Step three: Set aside a specific time every day to read God's Word and pray.**

Your constant fellowship and communion with the Lord is essential. It will keep you focused on the right path and alert you to any impending temptation.

**Step four: Have a continuing sexual relationship with your spouse.**

Intimacy doesn't have to die. Make the physical part of marriage intentional. Even in advancing years or times of sickness, you can still maintain an emotional closeness.

## SEVEN THINGS TO AVOID

As a married person, you are still going to relate constantly to the opposite sex in your work environment, school, sporting events, the grocery store and in a hundred other settings. In many cases you are well acquainted with these people, but you can know them in a holy and a righteous way.

Let me give you some practical advice. Here's what to avoid with someone of the opposite sex who is not your spouse:

**1. Avoid lunches or dinners together.**

Regardless of the reason, don't eat out alone with someone of the opposite sex who is not your spouse.

**2. Avoid private telephone conversations with the opposite sex.**

Except for short business calls, never engage in social or "small talk" with such a person.

### 3. Avoid questionable car pooling.

Don't be seen alone with a member of the opposite sex – just the two of you in the car. Simply set a personal standard that there will either be one person or three in the vehicle. The Bible says to *"Abstain from all appearance of evil"* (1 Thessalonians 5:22 KJV).

### 4. Avoid E-mail entanglements.

Pull the plug on those quick "just touching base" E-mails with someone of the opposite sex. Even change your Internet address if necessary. Yes, evil lurks in cybersapce!

### 5. Avoid intimate gifts of any kind to a person of the opposite sex who isn't in your family.

Giving something "personal" sends the wrong message. You're only asking for trouble even if your intention is innocent.

### 6. Avoid trips out of town for the day.

More than one married woman has heard a male boss say, "I've got an important meeting this afternoon and need you to take notes. It's only about two hours away."

Instead of responding, "Okay, let me get my notebook," say, "I don't travel with married men alone." If that's what is demanded by your employer, consider changing jobs!

**7. Avoid physical touching.**

*In one study, 20 percent of the men who were involved in adulterous affairs said it started by holding hands.*

You are walking down the street with a co-worker when a car zooms close to the curb. Suddenly, he or she is grabbing your hand, or protectively holding your body. Be careful!

In one study, 20 percent of the men who were involved in adulterous affairs said it began by hand-holding. The percentage was even higher for women.

**8. Don't ever confide in someone of the opposite sex about your personal marital troubles.**

"Hi, Marty. You'll never believe what Dave did the other night." That's the beginning of a conversation that could end in disaster.

## YOU CAN BE FREE!

You may say, "I know God's rules concerning adultery, yet I am still battling with the problem. How can I be free?"

**Confess your sin and repent before God.**

Be honest with yourself. Intimate relations outside the bonds of marriage is a sin! Bring it to the Lord in total repentance, asking Him to cleanse your mind, your heart and your body.

You will be able to say with David, *"I sought the Lord, and he answered me; he delivered me from all my fears"* (Psalms 34:4).

## Make a commitment that this behavior will end immediately!

Circle this day on your calendar and declare, "It's over!"

You may need to make a phone call or write a letter, yet whatever it takes, make up your mind you will never repeat an act of adultery again.

Tell God, tell yourself, then tell the other person. "No more!"

## Let God take care of this matter.

Because of your carnal nature, you find yourself in deep trouble. Do you tell the world, or confess it to the Lord?

Based on my years of ministry, I believe for all concerned, you should have conversations with only two people regarding the matter – the person with whom you had the affair (saying "It is over!) and God.

Here's what the Word says: *"It is the glory of God to conceal a matter; to search out a matter is the glory of kings"* (Proverbs 25:2).

Others may love to hear the salacious details: "Where did you go? What did you do? What did she say?" Suddenly a widening circle of people are feeding off of your sin.

Get your heart right with God and allow Him to take control. He will forgive, cleanse and cover you – enabling you to move on with your life.

Regardless of past mistakes, you can have a fresh start by making a promise to God and to your spouse you will honor for eternity!

---

### DECISIONS

*What does God say about intimate relations outside of marriage?*

*What are the danger signals that lead to adultery?*

*Specifically, what step will you take to strengthen your marriage?*

# DISCOVERY 8

# WHAT BELONGS TO OTHER'S IS THEIRS!

*He who steals an egg will steal a camel.*
— ARABIAN PROVERB

Our culture seems to be infatuated with stealing. If you've ever watched Gene Hackman in *Heist,* Mark Wahlberg in *The Italian Job* or George Cloony in *Oceans 11,* you know that Hollywood glorifies thievery. More than not, the audience finds itself rooting for the bad guys!

Stealing should bring shame, not applause.

What has society come to when it's okay for heros to get away with their crimes? It should not surprise us that we have raised a generation that doesn't bat an eye about cheating on exams or illegally downloading MP3 music from the Internet.

We can only imagine how disappointed God must be

since He wrote in the Eighth Commandment:

*You shall not steal.*
EXODUS 20:15

Allow me to tell you how this issue has personally affected me.

When Robyn and I were married in January, 1973, we lived in a sparsely furnished one bedroom apartment in Fort Worth, Texas. At least it had air conditioning and a swimming pool – great amenities for us.

We had been living there for about one year when my grandmother Holloway came for a visit. We thought she would be excited about the place, but when grandma stepped into our apartment, practically the first words out of her mouth were: "You're making a big mistake!"

"What are you talking about?" I asked, surprised.

Grandma shook her head and said, "You are throwing this rent money away every month. You're wasting it!"

At the time I was making $125 a week and the apartment was costing $140 each month – so the budget was tight.

"You need to own your own home," she persisted. All I could think of was my parent's beautiful home and I responded, "That's not possible!"

"Of course, it is," she lectured us. "You need to start building equity."

"Equity? I answered. "What's that?" I had never heard the word before.

She tried to explain the concept but I was having a

difficult time understanding. Since she was in real estate, I figured she knew what she was talking about.

"Stop renting," she insisted. "You're throwing your money down the drain!"

"Well, grandma," I said, "we only have about $500 saved from our wedding. How can we buy a house with that?"

"Don't worry about it," she replied. "Let's go looking for some property."

She took the wheel and started driving toward what I considered the wrong side of town – with some rather rundown property. "You don't mean for us to live here, do you?" I protested.

*"Stop renting," she repeated. "You're throwing your money down the drain!"*

"This is exactly where you should start," she insisted. You need to get some equity going – some *sweat* equity!"

We walked into a tiny three room run-down house in which you could hardly turn around. The price was $13,000 and they wanted $800 down.

Grandma said, "I have $300 to add to what you have. This will be a great place to get started with your equity." She *made* us buy the house.

### You've got to start somewhere!

The night we moved in, Robyn fell onto the bed and began sobbing. "I can't believe you brought me to this dump!" she cried.

"Well, dear," I responded, "I'm kind of surprised myself!" And I was.

What an exhausting time we had! I was taking college classes every morning, then working in ministry practically every afternoon and evening. We'd get home around 10:00 P.M. and work until two o'clock in the morning on that little dump – patching, painting and stripping the floors. Our new "wall-to-wall" carpet was actually remnants we bought for about $1 a square foot.

Robyn found some drapes and gave the place her finishing touches. Then, ten months later, we received a call to be a pastor in Sacramento, California.

The day after I accepted, we placed a three-line classified in the local paper advertising our house for sale. About 90 minutes after the ad came out, a woman called and said, "Don't sell the house till I get there."

She showed up and inquired, "How much do you want for it?"

"$17,500, I answered. She wrote her check on the spot.

After paying off our bills, we had $3,000 left over. "That's equity," I said to myself – mentally thanking grandma Holloway.

**Movin' on up!**

With a lesson learned, we put that money as a deposit on a $30,000 fixer-upper in Sacramento. Two years later we sold it and had $15,000 in equity to move into a better neighborhood – this time with our own pool in the back yard! And twenty-four months later, at the age of 27, we were sitting on $40,000 in equity.

That's when we were led of the Lord to go into full time evangelism. We sold the house, put our furniture in storage and moved to Tacoma, Washington, where we lived with Robyn's parents. That was our base as we traveled up and down the West Coast preaching the Gospel.

About six months later Robyn announced, "Guess what? We're going to be a mom and dad!"

My in-laws could handle two guests. But three? It was time to buy our own place and prepare for the baby's arrival.

We found a great home a few blocks away and moved our furniture from California.

### When everything is gone!

About three months after Jonfulton was born, I received a frantic call one morning from Robyn. She was at her mom's – where she always spent the night with the baby when I was out of town on a speaking engagement.

*"They've taken practically everything we own."*

"Honey, she began, sobbing. "Last night while I was at Mom's, burglars came and stripped our house clean. They've taken practically everything we own. They even screwed the light fixtures out of the ceiling."

She added, "The police told me this morning that it was a professional job. It probably didn't take them longer than 15 minutes."

I rushed to Tacoma and walked through a home that in the midnight hours had been plundered of everything valuable – things we had purchased with the profits from our "sweat equity" over the years. I felt dirty, violated and afraid.

*I felt dirty, violated and afraid.*

For the first time, I didn't feel secure in my own home. Since that experience, we've always had a burglar alarm system.

## EXCUSES DON'T COUNT

To my knowledge, the Tacoma thieves were never caught, but that doesn't mean they haven't been punished.

Many years later, as I was thinking about the robbery, I felt the Spirit of the Lord directing my attention to Jeremiah 17. As I began to read, this verse seemed to pop right off the page: *"Like a partridge that hatches eggs it did not lay is the man who gains riches by unjust means. When his life is half gone, they will desert him, and in the end he will prove to be a fool"* (Jeremiah 17:11).

The Lord spoke to me, "Rich, even though you never met the people who robbed you, I am telling you they have lost everything and are living the lives of a fool."

According to scripture, that is what every thief can look forward to.

If we could talk to those burglar's today, they would no doubt concoct an explanation to justify their behavior.

Here are five excuses many give for taking what doesn't belong to them:

1. "I deserve it – because I don't have it, and my friend *does*."
2. "I work here. They don't pay me what I am worth, so I'm just making up the difference."
3. "I was only going to borrow it!"
4. "It wasn't that much. What are you so upset about?"
5. "I just couldn't help myself."

No matter what the excuse, the bottom line is that God says, "Stealing is wrong! Don't do it!"

The Bible also talks specifically about the penalty. *"A thief must certainly make restitution, but if he has nothing, he must be sold to pay for his theft"* (Exodus 22:3). And if the stolen item is found in his possession, *"he must pay back double"* (v.4).

It's not enough to admit you are sorry; restitution is required. God told Moses to warn the Israelites, *"When a man or woman wrongs another in any way and so is unfaithful to the Lord, that person is guilty and must confess the sin he has committed. He must make full restitution for his wrong, add one fifth to it and give it all to the person he has wronged"* (Numbers 5:6-7).

In today's vernacular, God says if you rip someone off and then confess it to them, you are to reimburse the person for exactly what you took, plus 20 percent. And if you refuse to admit your guilt and are caught, you'll have to pay double.

God expects us to respect another person's property.

I have often listened to Dr. Laura Schlessinger on the

radio. She's a Jewish psychologist who takes a tough line on moral issues. To her, things are either right or wrong – there's nothing in between.

This is her philosophy on stealing: "If you haven't bought it, earned it, been given it, or inherited it, it belongs to someone else, and that's where it should stay."

**Everything will be revealed.**

The world of journalism was rocked when it was revealed that top reporters at the *New York Times* and *USA Today* were guilty of both plagiarizing and fabricating news stories – over a considerable period of time.

In the *Times* case, certain individuals knew what the writer was doing and warned two top executives at the paper, yet nothing was done. When the lying journalist was finally uncovered, the board of directors not only fired him – but the two executives are no longer with the paper.

Sooner or later, the deceiver is exposed.

On God's authority, I can say to every thief, con artist, rapist and murderer, no matter how much you try to conceal your crime, your sin will be revealed. The Bible says: *"...be sure your sin will find you out"* (Numbers 32:23 KJV).

## WHAT IS IN YOUR HAND?

Early in our ministry we met a young family who were committed to helping reach young people for Christ.

The father of the home was a giant of a man – about 6'6", 240 pounds. He was the quarterback on our flag football team, and a great golfer.

I mention this because he was missing four fingers on his left hand. So to drive a golf ball 320 yards and hit a softball over the fence with this physical handicap made him everybody's favorite. The students in our church loved both he and his wife.

I learned he had lost his fingers at the age of 16, when he was working part-time as a meat cutter, while still in high school.

It didn't seem to faze him – and he often told jokes about himself that made everyone laugh.

At a large retreat we organized for our youth group, this man and his wife volunteered to be part of the team. On the second night of the retreat, when I concluded the message, the convicting power of the Holy Spirit fell over the building and it was awesome. Over 100 young people literally *ran* to the altar – crying and confessing their sin to the Lord.

*He was broken before God and wept as I had never seen an adult weep before.*

In this inspiring service I saw this man walk down the aisle and throw himself over the altar. He was broken before God and wept as I had never seen an adult weep before.

When the altars began to clear, the man walked over to me and asked, "Rich, could I say something to these young people?"

I handed him the microphone, and through his sobs he said, "Only my wife and my high school boss know what I am about to share with you."

Immediately, a hush came across the audience. He

continued, "It's true I lost my fingers in a meat cutting accident, but me let tell you the rest of the story."

"Fourteen years ago I was working at a meat company. I'd been there for a year. The entire time I was stealing from my boss. I loved what the extra money I was taking from him could buy me."

The man had been raised in a Christian home and explained, "Over and over during that year the Lord was convicting me, saying, 'Give this up. Give this up!'"

The feeling intensified and God began to say, "If you don't change your ways I am going to make this sin public. Everyone you know will be aware of this."

He recalled, "I was stubborn, and kept on stealing."

*He recalled, "I was stubborn and kept on stealing."*

He then tearfully told us: "Late one night I was the only one working, cutting meat. Everybody else had left." And he said, "That night the knife slipped and I cut off my four fingers."

He told us that it wasn't God's will for this to happen, "But I had tempted and tested the Lord and continued to rebel against Him. God finally said, 'Okay. If that's what you want to do, I am going to let the whole world know what you have done."

He announced, "Tonight, I am publicly confessing. I have this left hand with no fingers because I stole from people and wasn't willing to make it right."

Sobbing deeply, he added, "I want to make restitution with my old boss – and with everybody."

The entire youth retreat made a circle around this man

and surrounded him with their prayers. It turned into a time of praise and celebration!

Today, he and his wife are in full-time ministry and having a great impact on thousands of lives.

You, too, may think you are taking something with your hand and getting away with it. It is not a secret with God.

If there's something in your life that has caused a barrier between you and the Master, why not settle it today?

## DOUBLE FORGIVENESS!

About three years into our evangelistic ministry on the West Coast, I was in a community where I spoke in several high schools during the week, culminating in a youth rally at a local church. The auditorium was jammed with students from those same schools.

My message that night was on the theme, "What you sow you are going to reap!" – and "Your sins will find you out."

As I came to the end of the sermon about 150 young people raised their hands indicating they wanted to make things right with God. Then, just as I was about to invite those same teens to come to the altar for prayer, suddenly a young man in the back of the auditorium bolted out of the row and ran out the back door. In an instant he was gone – and I wondered what on earth was happening. "I hope he's okay," I said to myself.

The altars were filled with people finding Christ as their Savior. Forty-five minutes later, most of the auditorium had cleared, but there were still a few praying at the front.

Again, the back door flung open and I saw the young man who had earlier fled the service. He came running down the center aisle and fell across the front of the stage, prostrate, and just bellowed, "Thank you, Lord! Thank you, Lord!"

I knelt beside him, laid my hand on his head and began to pray. The power of the Holy Spirit came upon this young man in an unusual way. What a joyous experience!.

**A cry for mercy.**

It was now about 10:30 P.M. Everyone was gone except for about four of the pastors. I helped the teen back on his feet and he told me his name – James.

I said, "Man, you really bolted out of here at the end of the service. Were you sick?"

He responded, "Yeah. I was sick and tired of being sick and tired."

"What happened?" I wanted to know.

He said, "Pastor Rich, I'm a senior in high school, and for three years I have worked six blocks from this church at a big grocery store." And he told us, "For the past three years, I've stolen from my boss – right out of the till. I devised a way it would never be discovered."

James continued, "I didn't think it was that bad, because I put in more hours than anyone else and the boss loved me. So I figured I deserved it."

Then, looking straight at me, he said, "But tonight, as you were preaching, a great fear came over me. It wasn't from the devil. It was from God."

He explained, "I could hear God saying to me, 'You'd better make this right.'" James also told us he wasn't raised in a home that knew much about the Lord – "But I knew without a doubt it was God talking to me."

"Pastor Rich," he said, "When you asked people to come to the altar, I hesitated. I didn't think I could ask God to forgive me when I knew my boss was down the street, working."

James described how he raced over to the grocery store, went to his employer's office and began to cry, telling him he'd just come from church. "I told him about my stealing and said, 'Sir, you can do whatever you want with me. I promise you, in time, I will pay everything back plus interest. If this isn't acceptable, just call the police and have them put me in jail. But I cannot ask God's forgiveness until I've asked you to forgive me. I want to make things right.'"

> *"Sir, you can do whatever you want with me."*

### Repayment? Restitution?

James told us, "I have never seen my boss so emotional. He began to cry, saying, "Son, let me tell you something. This company is so big across the country that we add into our budget the loss of money due to employee theft. It's already figured on the ledger.'"

Then his boss told him, "Of course, I have the right to fire you, or even call the police. But, James, I also have the choice to forgive you and let you keep working here. And that's exactly what I am going to do."

The manager looked at the young man and said, "In all my years of running stores, I've never had an employee come to me to confess a crime. I'm not a religious man, but I have never seen this before, and I believe something happened in your life tonight, James, and I am here to tell you that you are forgiven 100 percent. I don't require any repayment or restitution. I want to see you on the job tomorrow morning. Now get back to your church."

With a broad smile on his face, James exclaimed, "I came running back with this load off my shoulder, and when I reached this altar, God said, 'I forgive you, too.'"

Today, James and his entire family are serving the Lord.

**Removing the barrier.**

We've been talking about stealing, yet anything that has caused a rift between you and the Lord needs to be removed.

If the cistern of your soul is clogged because of your behavior, you can experience God's forgiveness this very moment. He will remove the sludge and sin from your life and cleanse your heart.

Don't wait another day to make things right with your fellow man – and with God. Remember, the Lord is just a prayer away.

## DECISIONS

*What excuses have you heard from those who have taken what doesn't belong to them?*

*How can parents teach the perils of stealing to their children?*

*Is there anything in your life for which you need to make restitution?*

# IF YOU WANT GOOD FRIENDS, ALWAYS TELL THE TRUTH

*Oh, what a tangled web we weave,*
*When first we practice to deceive.*

– SIR WALTER SCOTT

Let me tell you the story of a baker who was concerned that the farmer supplying him with butter was short-changing him. Upset, he began weighing the butter each week – and sure enough, discovered he was paying for a pound of butter but wasn't getting quite that much.

The furious baker had the man arrested and when the farmer stood before the judge, he was asked, "Sir, is it true you were short-changing the baker and selling him less than a pound of butter, yet charging him for a pound?"

The farmer replied, "Your Honor, I suppose it's true, but I was not aware of what I was doing. You see, on our farm we don't have scales. All we own is a balance, and so the only way I could measure a pound of butter was to put the baker's one-pound loaf of bread on the one side of the balance, and I kept filling the other side up with butter until it read a pound. I gave him what he gave me!"

The baker was guilty of more than fudging on the price of a loaf of bread, he was breaking the Ninth Commandment through deceit. God says:

> *You shall not give false*
> *testimony against your neighbor.*
> EXODUS 20:16

What does that mean? If you want good friends, "Don't lie!"

## Who do you trust?

It seems as a nation we can no longer handle the truth. In a *New York Times* poll, 91 percent of the respondents admitted they don't regularly speak the truth. And 20 percent said they don't go one day without lying about one thing or another.

Our current generation trusts the honesty of their grandparents much more than their peers. When asked, "Who do you trust to tell the truth? Today's young people replied:

- My grandparents: 79 percent of the time.
- My parents: 68 percent of the time.
- Me or my friends: 25 percent of the time.

Reversing that last statistic, young people believe they or their friends lie 75 percent of the time.

Whether you deliberately make an untrue statement, give a false impression or deceive, the intent is the same: you're lying!

God issued the Ninth Commandment because His kingdom is built on a foundation of truth, not deceit. The Bible says: *"Lying lips are an abomination to the Lord"* (Proberbs 12:22 KJV).

> *Whether you deliberately make an untrue statement, give a false impression or deceive, the intent is the same: you're lying!*

What we are discussing is more than a suggestion. God says truth-telling is a prerequisite for heaven. *"No one who practices deceit will dwell in my house; no one who speaks falsely will stand in my presence"* (Psalms 101:7).

Once, when Jehovah was speaking to Israel, He declared: *"Shall I acquit a man with dishonest scales, with a bag of false weights? Her rich men are violent; her people are liars and their tongues speak deceitfully. Therefore, I have begun to destroy you, to ruin you because of your sins"* (Micah 6:11-13).

The Lord is not passive on the issue of "bearing false witness." It is much more than a mere dislike. In the record of seven things God "hates" you'll find two involve this topic: *"a lying tongue"* (Proverbs:6:17) and *"a false witness that pours out lies"* (v.19).

> *One of the attributes of God is justice – He is honest, fair and just!*

Today, when we are surrounded with deception, people ask, "Why is lying such a big deal?

Let's get back to basics. One of the attributes of God is justice – He is honest, fair and just!

Most people don't expect better treatment than the next person; they only ask to be treated fairly and equitably. That is what the Lord insists upon, and why He can't tolerate deceit. You see, lying rips justice apart. It actually produces *injustice* – which results in human suffering, misery and even death.

## THE EXCEPTIONS

I've been asked, "Are there instances where it's okay to lie?"

If you look closely at scripture, all forms of lying are forbidden unless it is (1) to save a life, (2) foster justice or (3) demonstrate profound compassion and goodness to those who have been served injustice in their life.

Let me give you an example.

After David killed the giant, Goliath, his fame spread throughout the land and King Saul invited the popular hero to have dinner at the palace every night – and to be part of the family.

That's where David met Saul's oldest son, Jonathan. They became best friends and developed a great love for each other.

At the same time, King Saul grew extremely jealous of David – so much so that he conspired to kill the young man.

One day the Lord witnessed to David that Saul was about to take his life. He told Jonathan, "I know that if I show up at dinner tonight, your father is going to kill me. God told me. So instead, I'm going to hide in the field."

David told Jonathan to lie for him: *"If your father misses me at all, tell him, 'David earnestly asked my permission to hurry to Bethlehem, his hometown, because an annual sacrifice is being made there for his whole clan'"* (1 Samuel 20:6).

By not showing up for dinner, David thought Jonathan could himself learn what Saul's intentions were.

David said, "I'm so serious about this, that if you are on your father's side on this issue, then go ahead and kill me right now. I won't even put up a fight or argue. Just kill me."

Jonathan replied, "God forbid. I'll do what you ask."

That night there was an empty chair at the table. "Where is David?" King Saul demanded to know.

Jonathan told the lie – and Saul was so upset that he

121

sent his spies to find David so he could be killed.

Quietly, Jonathan left the table and warned David. "You're absolutely right. My father's out to take your life."

I believe this deceit was permitted by God to protect the line of the Messiah – and the Lord's plan for the ages.

## The scarlet thread.

Just before the great battle of Jericho, Joshua sent spies into the city to check out the territory prior to the attack.

When the men arrived, there was a harlot named Rahab waiting to help them.

She hid the spies in her home, and when the leaders of Jericho came to search her apartment, she said, "They were here, but they left." The truth was: *she had taken them up to the roof and hidden them under the stalks of flax she had laid out on the roof"* (Joshua 2:6).

The spies were grateful and told Rahab, "When we come in to attack, hold a scarlet thread out of your window. We'll see the thread and remember what you did for us – and we will spare you."

That's exactly what took place. When Israel came and destroyed Jericho, Rahab and her family were spared.

Again, I believe this woman of the street was allowed by God to use this deception because she too was in the line of David and a fore-mother of Jesus (Matthew 1:5).

If you have read *The Diary of Anne Frank* and *The Hiding Place* – the story of Corrie ten Boom, you'll learn how brave people hid Jews from Hitler's SS troops during World War II, protecting them from certain annihilation.

Was it wrong to tell the Nazi's "No there's no one here," to save innocent lives from injustice?

I believe this is where God grants an exception to His law against lying.

## SHAPING THE NEXT GENERATION

When the Almighty says "Do not lie," you know exactly what He is talking about – the deceit and misrepresentation that creeps into our everyday conversation, and the words we use to mislead and harm others.

By continuing as a nation down the path of perpetuating lies, the greatest at-risk group is our children. They are watching, listening and *copying* our behavior.

I keep thinking about this statement: What one generation condones, the next generation will openly practice.

*What one generation condones, the next generation will openly practice.*

To condone doesn't mean you necessarily agree – yet you allow others to practice the behavior.

Every person has a certain moral standard with outer limits they will not exceed. Your kids, however, start at your maximum point and push the envelope much further. That's why we must *"Train a child in the way he should go, and when he is old he will not turn from it"* (Proverbs 22:6).

Don't hesitate to surround your children with the truth of God's Word. I love it when I walk into a home and see a scripture verse framed on a wall! It's training that pays eternal dividends.

God says: *"These commandments that I give you today are to be upon your hearts. Impress them on your children. Talk about them when you sit at home and when you walk along the road, when you lie down and when you get up. Tie them as symbols on your hands and bind them on your foreheads. Write them on the doorframes of your houses and on your gates"* (Deuteronomy 6:6-9).

When you are fortunate enough to have a dinner-time conversation with your family, what's the topic of the day? Is it centered on the latest reality show on television? Do you talk about who's dating who in Hollywood?

As parents, we have an obligation to steer the conversation toward instilling principles of faith and belief – to discuss life issues in such a way they make a lasting impression on the minds and hearts of our children.

It may be as simple as talking about a story in the headlines – a CEO sentenced for embezzlement – a college coach charged in a "grade fixing" scandal. Then explain your opinion based on the teachings of God's Word. Ask your children, "What do you think about this?"

You might be surprised your children are paying such attention. In almost every instance, you'll find them repeating what you believe. Their own words will reinforce divine principles and shape their lives.

Character is created in childhood. That's why we need to do everything within our power to guide our sons and daughters in the right direction.

*Character is created in childhood.*

As King Solomon writes: *"Even a child is known by his actions, by whether his conduct is pure and right"* (Proverbs 20:11).

**The day I became a man.**

Constantly, I thank the Lord that I was raised by godly parents. I didn't learn lying and poor character in our home – it wasn't there!

Am I saying I was a perfect kid? Far from it!

I can clearly recall the day when at thirteen years of age I made a decision to deceive my dad. It was a serious lie.

At school one afternoon Mr. Sternburg, the home room teacher handed out report cards. We were to take them home, have the evaluation signed by our parents and returned the next day.

The moment I looked at the card, I knew I was in deep trouble. I'd gotten an "F" in Citizenship.

Still feeling the impact of the "D" I had received three months earlier, I found a pen and carefully changed the

"F" to a "B." Actually, it looked pretty authentic!

Mom and dad were overjoyed. "Son, we're so proud of you!" they exclaimed, giving me a big hug. "Way to go!"

*They signed the card, but now my head was spinning.*

They signed the card, but now my head was spinning. How was I going to change the letter back before handing it to the teacher? I found an eraser and frantically began to work on it. The more I scrubbed the messier it became. Frustrated, I finally, wrote the "F" – over a great big blotch.

I turned it in to Mr. Sternberg and he instantly said, "Wilkerson, it looks like you changed this grade here."

I said, "What? You've got to be kidding!"

The man repeated, "I can tell you changed this grade. What I want you to do is take this note home I'm writing to your father. Let him know that you lied to him. Then bring me the note with his signature tomorrow, I want to make sure he understands what you did."

Oh, boy! Hoping to delay the inevitable, I took the long route home that day. I wanted to see as much of the geography of the planet as possible before I went home to be with the Lord! Of course, I knew my dad would allow me to repent just before he took my life – so at least I would go to heaven!

As I walked in the house, my body was numb and I felt woozy, as if I was about to faint. Finally, somehow I summoned the courage to say, "Mom and dad. I've got some bad news for you."

"What is it?" they asked, with furrowed brows.

I looked down at the floor and mumbled, "I lied."

"Tell us about it," my dad insisted.

"Well," I began, "That "B" I got in Citizenship was actually an "F." I changed it before showing it to you."

My dad looked at me and said, "Go to your room, son." I knew what that meant!

In my bedroom, I didn't make a sound – just waited and waited and waited. That was the worst part – and my dad knew it. Oh, the remorse I felt for lying to my parents.

Then my imagination ran wild as I began to think of the upcoming punishment. Would it be napalm or a hand grenade? I thought "When he's finished with me . . ." – I couldn't even go there!

*"I'm sorry, son," he began. "I've failed you."*

Finally, dad walked in and sat down on the green chair across from me. He cradled his head in his hands and began to weep. "I'm sorry, son," he began. "I have failed you. You thought you had to lie to me to get my approval. Somewhere I made a mistake."

Now he was sobbing even harder.

"No, Dad!" I quickly reassured him. "It's all my fault. I'm the one who lied."

Then, to my surprise, he walked over and placed his

arms around my shoulders and told me how much he loved me.

"Rich," he said, "I'm not going to spank you, because today you have started on your journey toward manhood."

I was thirteen and said, "Really?"

"Yes, that's what I believe."

"Why do you say that?" I wanted to know.

I'll never forget his answer. "Son, no more can you ever find forgiveness at the end of my belt. You can't make up for what you've done anymore. From this day forward, I'm turning you over to your *Heavenly* Father." And he added, "You're going to find, son, that the Lord weeps more than I weep, because when you sin, you break His heart."

My dad was right. That was the day I started to become a man – and never had a spanking again. From that time forward, telling the truth and being a person of my word was seared into my spirit.

Oh, by the way, dad did make sure that I went to the school principal, the homeroom teacher – and every one of my teachers – the next day to ask their forgiveness for telling a lie. *I never forgot that!*

As parents, you have the golden opportunity to be the model of good character – and to imprint honesty and integrity on the hearts of your children.

Jesus said *"I am the way and the truth and the life"* (John 14:6). When you truly walk in His footsteps, there's no room for deceit.

---

### DECISIONS

*Do you believe God sees a difference between "shading the truth" and an outright lie?*

*How can you teach the principles of honest behavior to your children?*

*What commitment will you make to the Lord so that your words and actions truly represent Him?*

---

# RIGHT MOTIVES LEAD TO GREAT ACHIEVEMENTS!

*The truest mark of being born with*
*great qualities is being born without envy.*
– FRANÇOIS DE LA ROCHEFOUCAULD

I once heard about a mother who's little girl had collected a fair amount of money from the "tooth fairy." Every time her daughter Amy lost a tooth they would carefully place it in a small envelope and tuck it under the daughter's pillow.

To Amy's delight, in the morning, the tooth was gone and in its place was $2. It was exciting! After all, two dollars is a lot of money to a child. Well, that was true until the day Amy visited one of her friends – who bragged "I got $10 for my tooth!"

On hearing this, Amy ran to her friend's mother and

pleaded, "Mrs. Evans, would you mind doing me a big favor? Please call my mom and tell her which tooth fairy you use?"

Even at a young age we learn envy and jealousy – wanting what someone else has. That's what God calls "covetousness" – and He forbids it in the Tenth Commandment:

> *You shall not covet your neighbor's house.*
> *You shall not covet your neighbor's wife, or his*
> *manservant or maidservant, his ox or donkey, or*
> *anything that belongs to your neighbor.*
>
> EXODUS 20:17

No one really knows when desire turns into greed, and greed into sin, but it usually doesn't take long!

The motivation to covet is not birthed in the mind, rather it festers in the heart. And even though you may try to mask it, God sees your intentions. Remember, *"The Lord does not look at the things man looks at. Man looks at the outward appearance, but the Lord looks at the heart"* (1 Samuel 16:7).

What is coveting? To me, it is a person who *wants to want*. They crave more and more, saying, "I've just got to have it!" or "Now that is exactly what I need." Yet, they are never, ever satisfied.

The great business mogul, Andrew Carnegie, was once asked, "Sir, how much money is enough?"

Carnegie answered, "Just a little bit more."

His words mirror what King Solomon wrote centuries before: *"Whoever loves money never has money enough; whoever loves wealth is never satisfied with his income"* (Ecclesiastes 5:10).

I rarely meet men or women who are content with their present income. They are constantly thinking about a raise, a promotion or a bonus. Enough, it seems, is never enough!

## IT'S NOT YOURS!

The commandment God gave to Moses includes three key areas of a person's possessions. Here is what He orders us to stay away from:

**First: Don't covet your neighbor's house.**

The "house" represents a man's material "stuff." It encompasses not only the roof over your head, but the car you drive, the clothes you wear and the endless purchases you make.

If you're looking at your neighbor's driveway, envying his new Mercedes, the Lord is talking straight to you!

God's entire system of justice is based on rewards and punishment. It is also the foundation of how we live and

*If you're looking at your neighbor's driveway, envying his new Mercedes, the Lord is talking straight to you!*

133

work. For example, few would roll out of bed tomorrow at the crack of dawn and head for their job if they knew they wouldn't be paid. I've yet to hear a person admit, "I work for my boss because he such a wonderful person. It's not about the money."

Most of us don't have the luxury of being a volunteer. We expect a reward for our labor. That is as it should be since Jesus says, *"the worker deserves his wages"* (Luke 10:7).

A man's material possessions are a reward for his consistency, diligence, loyalty and the sweat of his brow. So, when you covet a person's possessions, you are robbing that individual of those reward-producing attributes.

If you desire to steal these characteristics, you are expressing a great deal about yourself – that you don't value your own abilities and worth. You're saying, "I don't want discipline and hard work in my life. It takes too long. I'll steal them instead."

> *The green-eyed monster has them tottering on the brink of bankruptcy.*

In addition, the question remains: how much is enough?

I know people drowning under the weight of debt for "stuff" they accumulated because they were just trying to "keep up with the Joneses." The green-eyed monster has them tottering on the brink of bankruptcy.

Don't be deluded by the myth of "the more I acquire

the happier I will be." It never works!

**Second: Don't covet your neighbor's wife.**

As part of the commandment, the Lord forbids desiring forbidden fruit. It has been the ruin of millions since the beginning of time – and I'm talking about more than Adam biting into an apple from the wrong tree!

During the reign of David, in the spring, when the kings usually went off to war, he stayed behind in Jerusalem and sent Joab out to lead the troops.

One evening David got up from his bed and walked around on the roof of the palace. Scripture records: *"From the roof he saw a woman bathing. The woman was very beautiful, and David sent someone to find out about her"* (2 Samuel 11:2-3).

The object of his desire was Bathsheba, the wife of Uriah the Hittite – one of David's mighty warriors.

As was the custom in those days, David had many concubines, but for some reason he allowed sin to overwhelm him and he coveted this married woman. Enough was not enough!

David sent messengers to bring Bathsheba to the palace. The Bible records that *"She came to him, and he slept with her"* (v.4).

What happened next? *"The woman conceived and sent word to David, saying, 'I am pregnant'"* (v.5).

To show you how sin begets sin, David conspired to

have Uriah, her husband, sent to the front lines of battle where he was killed by the enemy.

After a  time of mourning, David brought her to the palace, *"and she became his wife and bore him a son. But the thing David had done displeased the Lord"* (v.27).

Following this tragic event, violence, pain and suffering entered David's family for the rest of his kingship.

> *The sin of covetousness is not only abhorrent to God, but also to the innocent party.*

The sin of covetousness is not only abhorrent to God, but also to the innocent party. From Bible times until the present, the husband of a wife whose been taken by another man, rarely forgives that individual. For *"jealousy arouses a husband's fury, and he will show no mercy when he takes revenge"* (Proverbs 6:34).

Why such outrage? Not only does a husband love his wife and hates the thought of losing her, he's humiliated, plus it besmirches the family name and may bring the husband's ability to leave a legacy to a halt.

For all we know, Uriah's family name came to an abrupt end because King David succumbed to the desires of the flesh.

**Third: Don't covet your neighbor's employees.**

You don't hear the terms "manservant" and

"maidservant" thrown around today. Instead, successful men and women have talented people working for them called "employees" – and this commandment says those people shouldn't be enticed away.

I've known entrepreneurs who scheme to steal a valued employee from a competitor. At the highest levels of business, "head-hunters" are commissioned to do just that. In many cases, this is pure covetousness.

There are three possible causes:

1. Perhaps the offender is envious.
2. Maybe he is dissatisfied with his own lot in life.
3. He may hate a competitor so much that he wants him publicly humiliated.

Or, the motive may involve all three. Whatever the reason, it is wrong!

## DESTROY THE ROOT

You will never fulfill the Master's promise for your life until you settle the questions of the heart. What are the true motives behind our actions? What drives us to commit what we know is against the principles of God's commandments?

I believe the root of covetousness is hatred – a spirit from hell itself that causes a man or woman to want what is not theirs. Most people don't even realize the depth of their feeling since it has resided in their soul so long they are desensitized to its presence.

This condition also leads to a distorted view of achievement. The difference between what the world calls success and what the Lord calls it are as opposite as night and day. Society says we win when we accumulate more "stuff":

- To have a model family, even if you have to steal someone else's.
- To have a successful company, even though you built it through hostile takeovers.

You may own a luxurious home on the top of a mountain and have a Lamborghini parked in the garage, but what's the advantage if your gains are at the expense of others and your heart finds no peace.

The only answer for jealousy and hatred is to ask God to replace those things with His deep, abiding love – for the Lord, yourself and your neighbor. The Bible tells us: *"Hatred stirs up dissension, but love covers over all wrongs"* (Proverbs 10:12).

With a change of heart, you can begin to experience true success. Years ago, an unknown person wrote these words:

> *Success is speaking words of praise,*
> *In cheering other people's ways,*
> *In doing just the best you can,*

RIGHT MOTIVES LEAD TO GREAT ACHIEVEMENTS!

*With every task and every plan,*
*It's silence when your speech would hurt,*
*Politeness when your neighbor's curt,*
*It's deafness when the scandal flows,*
*And sympathy with others' woes,*
*It's loyalty when duty calls,*
*It's courage when disaster falls,*
*It's patience when the hours are long,*
*It's found in laughter and in song,*
*It's in the silent time of prayer,*
*In happiness and in despair,*
*In all of life and nothing less,*
*We find the thing we call success.*

The apostle Paul expresses the same sentiment when he says: *"I have learned the secret of being content in any and every situation, whether well fed or hungry, whether living in plenty or in want. I can do everything through him who gives me strength"* (Philippians 4:12-13).

## Something worth desiring.

The only thing worth coveting is a personal relationship with the Lord. As David writes: *"One thing I ask of the Lord, this is what I seek: that I may dwell in the house of the Lord all the days of my life, to gaze upon the beauty of the Lord and to seek him in his temple"* (Psalms 27:4).

Develop a passion to be in God's presence, saying, "Lord, I want more of You."

## Your Greatest Discovery

The most important breakthrough you'll ever make on your road to achievement is to know that God loves you so much He sent His Son to earth – to be born as a Man, yet to die on a Cross for your sin. His blood was shed to cleanse your heart and prepare you for an eternity with Him.

Right now, you can receive Christ as your personal Savior. Ask Him to forgive and cleanse you, then make Him the Lord of your life.

I love the words of a song by Lanny Wolfe:

> *Only Jesus can satisfy your soul,*
> *And only He can change your heart and make*
> *    you whole;*
> *He'll give you peace you never knew,*
> *Sweet love and joy, and heaven too.*
> *For only Jesus can satisfy your soul!*

Friend, it is totally impossible to obey the TEN COMMANDMENTS on your own. Yet with God at the helm, you'll find strength beyond your own to abide by His covenants and to fulfil His promise for your future.

I am praying you will experience His amazing love

today. It's a life-changing discovery!

DECISIONS

*Can you name something you have coveted, yet not actually needed?*

*How do you cope with feelings of envy and jealousy in your own life?*

*What covenant will you make with the Lord to keep His commandments?*

# GOD'S PROMISE FOR MY FUTURE

According to Genesis 1:26-27

_____

(your first name)

## *was born for greatness...*

*Therefore...*

I CHOOSE to let go of my excuses so that God can work His greatness in my life. – Philippians 3:13

I CHOOSE to focus on my Lord and Savior Jesus Christ who STEPPED DOWN...so that I could STEP UP! – 2 Corinthians 8:9

I CHOOSE to "face my fears" in order to turn my potential for greatness into reality. – Mark 5:25-34

I CHOOSE today, once again, to move toward my great, victorious future. – Jeremiah 29:11

Signature: _____

FOR A COMPLETE LIST OF BOOKS,
TAPES AND MEDIA MATERIALS BY
RICH WILKERSON

CONTACT:

PEACEMAKERS
P. O. BOX 680100
MIAMI, FL 33168

PHONE: 305-749-0190
INTERNET: www.peacemakers.com

# ACKNOWLEDGMENTS

– To our Trinity Church family here in the *poorest* big city of America, Miami, Florida. As we always say: "We go one, we go all!"

– To the wonderful staff of men and women who serve with me in Miami in order to win the lost, help the poor and teach abundant living.

– To Dr. Laura Schlessinger. Her book on the Ten Commandments is the best I've ever read. Make sure you have a copy in your library.

– To my four sons, Johfulton, Rich, Jr., Graham and Taylor, who have been my laboratory for proving the 10 DISCOVERIES are the key to greatness.

– And finally, to my wife, Robyn. Since 1973 she has daily tested the 10 DISCOVERIES in my life. I love her with all my heart.